REGIONAL RURAL BANKS IN INDIA

CHALLENGES AND PROSPECTS

REGIONAL RURAL BANKS IN INDIA

CHALLENGES AND PROSPECTS

Edited by

Dr. Shaikh Sirajuddin

Delta Book World

New Delhi-110 002

First Published in 2017
ISBN 978-93-85719-03-5

Published by Abhishek Goel on behalf of
Delta Book World
G-4, Prahlad House
4832/24, Ansari Road
New Delhi - 110 002 (India)
Tel.: 011-2328 8140, 2324 5799
E-mail: deltabookworld@gmail.com

PRINTED IN INDIA

Dedicated to

Late Shaikh Alauddin, my father

and

Late Doulatannesa Bibi, my mother

Whose sacrifices and blessings
are my perennial sources of inspiration

Preface

The Department of Commerce of Saldiha College, Saldiha, Bankura organized a UGC sponsored national seminar on November 16-17, 2016 on the theme "Regional Rural Banks in India: Challenges and Prospects." The Seminar was attended by delegates and resource persons coming from different colleges and universities of West Bengal and other states of India. A good number of papers were presented in the technical sessions of the seminar. From among the papers presented, seventeen papers were selected and sent to the referees for review and editing. After receiving green signals from the referees the papers are now being published in this volume.

The present volume with the title theme "Regional Rural Banks in India: Challenges and Prospects" is an attempt to place before the general readers the deliberations of the seminar in terms of the papers presented in the seminar.

It is hoped that this edited volume will not only provide good reading material on regional rural banks but also help the students, teachers and researchers for a better understanding of the issues involved and will help the government and policy makers to take better decisions in the present economic environment. The major contribution of these articles is available in a summarized form from the introduction which follows.

The editor would like to thank the contributors without whose cooperation this volume could not be published in time. The editor is also grateful to the referees who have made extremely valuable suggestions and have thus contributed in enhancing the quality of the volume. The editor is equally grateful to the publisher for his cooperation and help to publish this in an elegant manner. The University Grants Commission must also be thanked for granting financial assistance for organizing the seminar and for the publication of the edited volume. The editor expresses a deep sense of gratitude and obligation to his teacher and research guide, Professor Jaydeb Sarkhel, Former Professor, Department of Commerce, The University of

Burdwan for his wise and valuable guidance and unflinching encouragement at every stage of preparing this volume. The editor also acknowledges his indebtedness to Professor Chittaranjan Sarkar and Professor Debasish Sur of the Department of Commerce of The University of Burdwan who have provided the necessary stimulus for publishing this edited volume.

Lastly, the editor thanks the teachers of the college as well as the office staff of the college for their whole hearted cooperation in bringing out this volume. Needless to say, any deficiency that remains is due to the editor's fault.

Dr. Shaikh Sirajuddin
Principal, Saldiha College,
Saldiha, Bankura, West Bengal

Contents

Abbreviations

AEPS	:	Adhaar Enabled Payment System
APL	:	Above Poverty Line
BCAs	:	Business Correspondent Agents
BIRD	:	Banker's Institute for Rural Development
BMR	:	Bharat Microfinance Report
BP	:	Branch penetration
BPL	:	Below Poverty Line
BSRB	:	Banking Service Recruitment Board
CAB	:	College of Agricultural Banking
CAMELS	:	Capital, Asset Quality, Management, Earnings, Liquidity, and Sensitivity
CDR	:	Credit Deposit Ratio
CP	:	Credit Penetration
CRAR	:	Capital to Risk weighted Assets Ratio
CRISIL	:	Credit Rating Information Services of India Limited
CRR	:	Cash Reserve Ratio
CSC	:	Common Services Centre
DAP	:	Development Action Plan
DBT	:	Direct Benefit Transfers
DC	:	Diversification Consumption

DCB	:	Demand Collection Balance
DICGC	:	Deposit Insurance and Credit Guarantee Corporation
DO	:	Demand Order
DP	:	Deposit Penetration
DRDC	:	The District Rural Development Cell
DRI	:	Differential Rate of Interest
EBTs	:	Electronic Benefit Transfers
EEA	:	Expansion of Economic Activities
FICCI	:	The Federation of Indian Chambers of Commerce and Industry
FII	:	Financial Inclusion Index
FIP	:	Financial Inclusion Plan
FITF	:	Financial Inclusion and Technology Fund
FSS	:	Farmers' Service Society
GCC	:	General Credit Cards
GEL	:	Granting Education Loan
GNPA	:	Good Neighbors Planning Alliance
GOI	:	Government of India
IBA	:	India Banks' Association
IBPS	:	Institute of Banking Personnel Selection
IDBI	:	Industrial Development Bank of India
IRDP	:	Integrated Rural Development Programme
IRDR	:	Indian Rural Development Report
KCC	:	Kishan Credit Card
KYC	:	Know- Your- Customer
MCR	:	Magstripe Card Reader

MFIs	:	Micro Finance Institutions
MGNREGA	:	Mahatma Gandhi National Rural Employment Guarantee Act
MS	:	Mobilisation of Savings
NA	:	Not Available
NABARD	:	National Bank for Agriculture and Rural Development
NHB	:	National Housing Bank
NIBM	:	National Institute for Bank Management
NIT	:	National Industrial Tribunal
NPAR	:	Non-Performing Asset Ratio
NPAs	:	Nonperforming Assets
NREP	:	National Rural Employment Programme
NSSO	:	National Sample Survey Organisation
OPCE	:	Organization of the Petroleum Exporting Countries
OPR	:	Overnight Policy Rate
PACS	:	Primary Agricultural Credit Societies
PBH	:	Promotion of Banking Habits
PBS	:	Performance Budgeting System
PCA	:	Principal Component Analysis
PCR	:	Provision Coverage Ratio
PMJDY	:	Pradhan Mantri Jan – Dhan Yojana
PMRGY	:	Prime Minister's Employment Generation Programme
PPP	:	Public-Private-Partnership
POS	:	Point of Sale
PSBs	:	Public Sector Banks

RBI	:	Reserve Bank of India
ROAR	:	Return On Assets Ratio
RRBs	:	Regional Rural Banks
RTGS	:	Real Time Gross Settlement
SBI	:	State Bank of India
SD	:	Standard Deviation
SGSY	:	Swarnajayanti Gram Swarojgar Yojana
SHGs	:	Self-Help Groups
SIDBI	:	Small Industries Development Bank of India
SLR	:	Statutory Liquidity Ratio
STFL	:	Short Term Farmer's Loan
TRIPS	:	Trade Related Intellectual Property Rights System
UBI	:	United Bank of India
UNDP	:	United Nations Development Programme
UP	:	Uttar Pradesh
USBs	:	Ultra Small Branches
VLEs	:	Virtual Learning Environments
VSAT	:	Very Small Aperture Terminal

Introduction

The present book is the outgrowth of a national seminar organized by the Department of Commerce, Saldiha College in November 2016 on the theme 'Regional Rural Banks in India: Challenges and prospects' where different scholars have focused on different aspects of the functioning of rural banks (RBs) in India. The book consists of seventeen research papers where the authors have highlighted different issue relating to RRBs in India. This introduction provides a brief summary of the papers published in this book.

The paper by Dr. Siddhartha Bhadra and Dr. Debasish Biswas makes a critical review of the performance of RRBs in India. They have analysed the growth of RRBs from the view point of rural development. It focuses the role of RRBs since their inception in rural development and evaluates their role in recent times at the changing paradigm of the Indian rural economy. It highlights the recent problems of RRBs and also provides some suggestions for improvement of their functions for rural development.

Dr. Santosh Koner and Prof. Jaydeb Sarkhel in their paper have given an outline of the growth of RRBs in India. It examines why the RRBs lost their focus by outlining the problems faced by the RRBs. It gives an account of recommendations of different committees set up from time to time to consider the problems of RRBs. The paper also gives several suggestions for making the RRBs more viable.

In their joint paper Dr. Debasish Sur and Dr. Dhanonjoy Kumar provide an alternative approach for the measurement of risks of RRBs in India. It narrates different components of risks and considers the measurement of risks of RRBs. Apart from the non statistical CAMEL measure it also considers statistical measures involving coefficient of variation of different relevant ratios. It also provides an alternative measure of risks based on Ginni coefficient of concentration and Ginni coefficient of mean difference. The paper is theoretical in nature.

Dr. Uttam Kumar Dutta in his paper gives an overview of the role of RRBs in the economic development of rural India. The paper starts with the findings of the India Rural Development Report (2012-13) and highlights poverty concentration in certain regions and social groups. It then considers some operational activities of RRBs in India like expansion of branches, agricultural credit flow, opening of no-frills accounts, achievement under PMJDY, recovery performance etc. It also gives an account of the problems faced by the RRBs and some suggestions to overcome these problems.

Dr. Chittaranjan Sarkar in his paper has taken up the role of RRBs in the socio-economic development of India. He has also considered the financial performance of RRBs. He has emphasized the conduction of CSR activities of companies through RRBs in order to make the RRBs viable.

Dr. Samirendra Nath Dhar and Prof. Pintu Prasad Jaiswal in their joint paper have considered the business correspondent agent model of financial inclusion. They have made a case study of Sikkim in the post demonetisation period. First of all they give an outline of the business correspondent agent model of financial inclusion and then they point out the hindrances in operations of the business correspondent agents. They then narrate three cases of business correspondent agents in Sikkim. The paper concludes by pointing out some of the difficulties faced by business correspondent agents in Sikkim.

Dr. Krishna Singh in his paper made an empirical assessment of financial inclusion achieved through RRBs in India. He starts with the definition of financial inclusion and provides a review of related literature. He then develops a financial inclusion index through the application of principal component method. He also analyses the observed financial inclusion scenario across the states in India.

Prof. Swapan Kumar Biswas has made a comparative study of the performance of RRBs in India. He takes two time periods - the pre-amalgamation period and the post-amalgamation period and makes a comparative study of the performance of RRBs in these two periods. In this process he has taken several parameters such as growth of branches, fund component, deposit mobilization, loans and advances made, recovery rate, maintenance of CRAR and profitability and viability of RRBs. He also provides some suggestions and recommendations for the improvement in the performance of RRBs in India.

In their joint paper Prof. Goutam Sinha, Dr. Goutam Chatterjee and Dr. Uday Chand Das have considered the management of nonperforming assets (NPAs) of RRBs in India. They first give the definition of NPAs and mention the direct and indirect impacts of NPAs. They show the trend of NPAs in RRBs and compare them with that of nationalised commercial banks in India during the period 2004-05 to 2013-14 by using secondary data. It is concluded that the size of NPAs of RRBs is gradually increasing and the rate of growth is also increasing. The same picture is also found in case of nationalised commercial banks in India.

Prof Partha Pratim Roy has examined the functioning of RRBs in India in the context of financial sector reforms. The paper outlines the features of RRBs during the reform period. It also shows the changing objectives and mode of functioning of RRBs from the pre-reform period to the post - reform period.

Dr. Tanay Kumar Pal and Prof Dhiren Pal in their joint paper give an overview of the problems and prospects of RRBs in India. The paper starts with the concept and genesis of RRBs in India. It highlights the role of RRBs as an agency of creating banking habits among rural people. The paper also lists the problems faced by the RRBs and offers some suggestions for strengthening the position of RRBs in India

Dr. Sk. Ataur Rahaman in his paper has considered the role of RRBs in financial inclusion in India. It shows how the RRBs have performed recently and how the RRBs are trying to enlarge financial inclusion by taking different initiatives.

Dr. Pankaj Kumar Pal has conducted a field survey among the students of a few colleges in Paschim Medinipur district of West Bengal regarding the awareness of the students about the role of RRBs in rural development. The findings of the field survey are given in his paper. The study covers 710 students belonging to BPL and APL families residing in rural and urban areas. The findings reveal that there is no discrepancy in the opinion about the positive association between RRBs and rural development. However, there exists some variation regarding the attitude about awareness towards the role of RRBs on rural development among the respondents belonging to different socio-economic status, localities and gender.

Prof Ratul Saha, Prof. Bhajan Chandra Barman and Dr. Arun Kumar Roy in their joint paper consider the role of RRBs in micro finance. The paper makes an attempt to make an evaluative study of the performance of RRBs in the field of microfinance under SGSY in two districts of West Bengal-Coochbehar and Bankura. The study comes to conclude that although RRBs play vital role in rural microfinance but the SHG movement by RRB is not uniform across the districts of West Bengal. Bankura is lagging behind Coochbehar in all respects of the chosen indicators of growth of SHGs.

Prof. Subrata Jana, Dr. Sukhen Kali and Dr. Rabindranath De Dalal in their joint paper have considered the problems and the current scenario of RRBs in India. They have considered the structure of agricultural credit system in India and the place of RRBs in this structure. The paper outlines the major problems faced by RRBs. It also gives some performance indicators of RRBs while dealing with the present scenario.

Dr. Probhat Kumar Pal in his paper considers the financial viability and potentiality of RRBs in India by taking into consideration the long term and short term liquidity of RRBs, profitability of the RRBs and amount of loan extended to the small and marginal farmers. The study also explains the profitability of the RRBs, comparative rate of growth of owned capital, debt capital, total capital and net profit. Relationship between debt capital and net profit, owned capital and net profit are also measured in this study.

Dr. Mantu Kumar Das in his paper has considered the challenges and prospects of RRBs in India. The paper argues that most of the rural areas of India are now covered by RRBs through their largest network. The success of rural credit in India largely depends on their financial strength. RRBs are the key financing institutions at the rural level which shoulders responsibility of meeting credit needs of the agricultural sector. However the RRBs are faced with several problems at present- such as problems of overdue, non recovery of advances, nonperforming assets and other problems.

1

Performance of Regional Rural Banks (RRBS) in India:
A Critical Overview

Siddhartha Bhadra
Debasish Biswas

INTRODUCTION

India is a country of villages where about 70% of the total population is living in rural areas. So development of India is only possible by the development of the people living in rural areas. Most of those rural people are facing various problems such as poverty, unemployment, housing, illiteracy etc. Those problems can be removed only through the development of rural area and for which substantial credit is essential. The co-operative and commercial banks made considerable progress in providing credit to rural development. But, those banks are suffering from many weaknesses. In order to improve supply of rural credit RRBs were established in 1975. The roles of these banks are complimentary and supplementary along with the co-operative and commercial banks. Development of agricultural and non-agricultural productive activities of the rural areas is the main objective of supplying credit by the RRBs. In 1975, five regional rural banks were established in different places such as at Gorakhpur and Moradabad in Uttar Pradesh, Jaipur in Rajasthan, Bhiwani in Haryana and Malda in West

Bengal under the sponsorship of State Bank of India, the Syndicate Bank, United Commercial Bank, Punjab National Bank and United Bank of India respectively.

The RRBs are playing a very important role for all-round development of rural areas of the country. In recent years, Regional Rural Banks have been set up all over the country. Now, these Banks have been receiving a high importance in the rural credit system. But the most RRBs are making losses. The RRBs would lend only to the weaker sections of rural society, offering lower interest rates, expanding branches in remote and rural areas. But the profit motivation was absent. The Credit Deposit Ratio of the banks continuously decreased. Now, the viability of these banks is a matter of concern. RRBs are suffering from the mounting losses due to unwise commercial policy.

OBJECTIVES

This article concentrates on the role of the Regional Rural Banks for the upliftment of the rural areas of India. It wants to analyse the contribution of RRBs towards fulfilling the objectives of enrichment and betterment of the overall quality of the rural life through the development of agriculture, trade, commerce, industry and other usual productive activities in different village areas of the country.

The purpose of this research is to examine the challenges, opportunities and constraints faced by the RRBs in the development of Indian Rural Economy through rural credit.

RESEARCH METHODOLOGY

This research is based on secondary data and information. The data have been collected from different reports, journals, websites and existing literatures.

LITERATURE REVIEW

A number of studies describe the functioning and performance of RRBs in India. Some of those studies which are relevant for this research are as follows.

M.K. Jain[1] made a noteworthy study entitled "Role of RRBs in the development of India". This study showed the role and problems of RRBs in the development of rural economy and suggested some measures for its improvement.

M. Chakrabarti's[2] study on the role of RRBs in West Bengal state in India in financial inclusion exhibit various banking services of RRBs in West Bengal. He shows these banks are playing a significant role in ensuring sustainable development through financial inclusion. He suggested for expansion of RRBs network to benefit the rural people through broader banking services.

J.K. Ram[3] analyses the genesis, growth and performance of the RRBs in India from 1975 to 2014. This Study exhibits the progress of RRBs in India and gives valuable suggestions for the restructuring of the RRBs.

PERFORMANCE

The RRBs are owned by three institutions and their shares are as follows:

- Central Government → 50%
- State government → 15%
- Sponsor bank → 35%

The first RRB was "Prathama Bank" in Muradabad district of Uttar Pradesh. Simultaniously four other RRBs were established in Jaipur in Rajasthan, Gorakhpur in UP, Malda in West Bengal and Bhiwani in Haryana. Since their inception, the number of RRBs and their branches grew rapidly and it covered large number of districts in India. On 31 March, 2004, the number of RRBs was 196, number of their branches was 14,446 and the number of their covering districts was 518. The growth of RRBs can be shown by the Table-1.

Table-1: Performance of RRBs in India

Year	No. of RRBs	Dist. Covered	Branches
1975	6	12	17
1976	40	84	489
1977	48	99	1187
1978	51	102	1753
1979	60	111	2420
1980	73	130	2735
1981	102	167	3784
1982	121	207	5393

Year	No. of RRBs	Dist. Covered	Branches
1983	142	249	6812
1984	162	286	8727
1985	183	322	12139
1986	194	343	12755
1987	196	362	13076
1988	196	365	13586
1989	196	369	14079
1990	196	372	14443
1991	196	381	14527
1992	196	392	14539
1993	196	398	14543
1994	196	408	14542
1995	196	425	14509
1996	196	427	14497
1997	196	427	14461
1998	196	451	14475
1999	196	484	14499
2000	196	484	14301
2001	196	500	14313
2002	196	511	14390
2003	196	516	14433

Source: statistics on RRBs, published by NABARD

Since 2005, the government of India started amalgamation of RRBs sponsored by the same bank within a state. After the amalgamation, the numbers of RRBs were decreased gradually from 196 to 133 in 2006, to 64 in 2013, to 57 in 2014 and to 56 in 2016.

DEPOSIT MOBILIZATION

Deposit mobilization is required for the credit expansion of the RRBs. These banks encourage the people of rural area to save more through the various deposit schemes.

Demand Deposits schemes

- **Saving Bank accounts:** Regular deposit scheme for all customers including borrowers

- **No frills savings accounts**
- **Current Account:** Multiple deposit and withdrawals for institutions
- **Jeeva Nidhi:** accidental insurance for which Premium is paid out of the interest earned from SB account

Term Deposits schemes

- Fixed Deposit (6 – 120 months): Small amounts starting from Rs. 100
- Recurring Deposit (6 – 120 months): Minimum amount will be Rs. 50 per month

Awareness Programmes for Savings Mobilization by RRBs

- **Quarterly village level awareness campaign:** to explain importance of savings and features of different savings products by the bank officials such as
- village meetings
- distribution of leaf lets
- giving information on savings product
- **Observes special deposit mobilization fortnight with special schemes**

The following table exhibits the amount of deposit mobilization of RRBs during 1990 to 2001.

Table – 2: YEAR-WISE DEPOSIT MOBILISATION BY RRBs

(Rupees in Crore)

Year at the end of	Total Deposits	Average per RRBs	Average per Branch	Percentage variation of Total Deposits
March – 91	4989.24	25.46	0.34	-
March – 92	5867.83	29.98	0.40	17.61
March – 93	6938.13	35.40	0.48	18.25
March – 94	8826.51	45.03	**0.61**	27.22
March – 95	11150.01	56.89	**0.72**	26.33
March – 96	14187.90	72.39	0.98	27.25
March – 97	17970.18	91.68	**1.24**	26.67
March – 98	22189.23	113.21	**1.53**	23.48
March – 99	27065.74	138.09	1.87	21.98
March – 2000	32204.35	164.31	2.25	19.00
March – 2001	38277.78	195.29	2.67	18.86

Source: Statistics on the Regional Rural Banks for the period: 1991-2001, NABARD

From table – 1, we see that total deposits of RRBs gradually increased during 1990 – 2001. But the growth rate was fluctuating. Since 1996 growth rate gradually diminished. Both average deposit per RRBs and average deposit per branch gradually increased during the period.

The amount of total deposit increased gradually throughout the period.The amount of deposit in 1991 was Rs. 4989.24 crore, which increased to Rs. 211458.32 crore in 2013.

ADVANCES

A large portion of the rural population needs bank loan for agricultural and non-agricultural activities. The poor farmers and even big farmers need credit at reasonable cost to purchase modern machines and to meet other agricultural cost. RRBs provide credit to those farmers. Table – 2 shows the deployment of credit by the RRBs in rural areas during 1991 - 2001.

Table – 3: Years-Wise Outstanding Advances by RRBs
(Rupees in Crore)

Year at the end of	Total Advances	Average per RRBs	Average per Branch	Percentage variation of Total Advances
March – 91	3535.35	18.41	0.25	-
March – 92	4090.86	29.87	0.28	15.17
March – 93	4626.73	23.61	0.32	11.58
March – 94	5253.02	26.80	0.36	13.54
March – 95	6290.27	32.10	0.43	19.75
March – 96	7505.03	38.29	0.52	19.31
March – 97	8711.82	44.45	0.60	16.08
March – 98	9868.81	50.31	0.68	13.19
March – 99	11355.84	57.94	0.78	15.16
March – 2000	13184.40	67.27	0.92	16.10
March – 2001	15814.89	80.67	1.11	19.95

Source: Statistics on Regional Rural Banks from 1991-2001, NABARD

Total advances given by the RRBs to the rural sector gradually increased during the period. The rate of growth during the period shows an increasing trend. The average advances per RRB and per branch also gradually increased.

CREDIT DEPOSIT RATIO (CDR)

The CDR of the RRBs gradually diminished. Table – 3 shows the CDR of RRBs during 1991 – 2001.

Table -4: Credit - Deposit Ratio

Year at the end of	CDR in %
March – 91	72
March – 92	70
March – 93	67
March – 94	60
March – 95	56
March – 96	53
March – 97	48
March – 98	44
March – 99	42
March – 2000	41
March – 2001	41

Source: Statistics of RRBs from 1991-2001 - NABARD

As CDR decreased continuously during the period we can say that the RRBs have failed to provide more credit compared to deposit.

RECOVERY

In rural area credit recoveries is a very difficult task. By the application of appropriate strategies of the RRBs, the recovery performance has been improved over the period 1991 – 2001. This is shown by Table – 4.

Table – 5: Recovery Performance of RRBs

Year at the end of	Demand	Collection	Balance	Percent of Recovery to Demand
June - 1991	2332.83	1054.59	1278.24	45.21
June - 1992	2395.78	979.62	1416.16	40.89
June - 1993	2726.25	1123.49	1603.16	41.20
June - 1994	3159.95	1460.85	1699.10	46.23

Contd...

Year at the end of	Demand	Collection	Balance	Percent of Recovery to Demand
June - 1995	3669.07	1870.36	1798.71	50.98
June - 1996	4426.88	2439.18	1987.70	55.10
June - 1997	5521.73	3144.91	2376.82	56.96
June - 1998	5916.63	3575.51	2341.12	60.43
June - 1999	6936.86	4445.98	2490.88	64.09
June - 2000	8690.79	6000.17	2690.62	69.04
June - 2001	NA.	NA.	NA.	NA.

Source: statistics of RRBs - NABARD

NA=Not Available

From Table – 4 we see a continuous increasing trend in recovery of the RRBs which indicates their success in this field.

DIFFERENT COMMITTEE REPORTS ON RRBS

RRBs faced huge losses and their role in rural development was far from satisfactory. To evaluate the performance of RRBs and to recommend measures a number of committees were appointed by the government and RBI form time to time.

The **Dantwala committee** (1978) appreciated the performance of RRBs and suggested that more and more RRBs should be established in non-bank areas to make RRBs an integral part of the rural credit.

The Kelkar Committee (1986) recommended for enhancement of authorized capital and paid up share capital of RRBs, more inspection of activities and verification of internal audit of RRBs by the sponsor banks and amalgamation of RRBs if required.

Agriculture Finance Corporation has made a study in 1986 on RRBs viability which was published by NABARD. That study exhibited the following

The two factors percentage of establishment costs in total cost and expansion of branches affected RRBs viability. RRBs suffered from losses due to defects in their systems and rectifications were essential. According to the study development of infrastructure facilities and opening of branches by commercial banks where there existed RRBs branches were required.

Agricultural Credit Review Committee- Khusro Committee (1989) showed the following problems of RRBs limited business flexibility with very low scope of expansion or diversification loans were small in size and risk-prone

The committee suggested the RBI to allow the RRBs to lend to non-target groups and to deregulate their deposit and lending rates. That is, the RBI should give more freedom to RRBs for investment of their surplus funds into profitable channel.

Narasimham Committee (1991) highlighted the followings poor financial health of the RRBs 172 of the 196 RRBS were unprofitable with an aggregate loan recovery 40.8 percent (June 1993).

According to the committee, the RBI should allow RRBs to engage in all types of banking business with targeted and non-targeted groups.

Vyas committee (2004) Suggested structural consolidation of RRBs by amalgamating RRBs sponsored by the same bank within a state.

The government of India followed the recommendation Vyas Committee and started the process of merger of RRBs sponsored by the same bank within a state. After the amalgamation, the numbers of RRBs were decreased from 196 to 133 as 31st March 2006 and further decreases from 133 to 64 as on 31st March 2013.

FINDINGS

- the penetration of Regional Rural Bank has been good in terms of opening of bank accounts
- very low amount of term deposit: because the rural poor people want regular income flow and they have preference for easy liquidity rather than expecting good return on the deposit amount
- the lack of sufficient promotional efforts by bank for promoting term deposits could be the other reason for less preference for term deposit
- most of the bank branches are concentrated at bigger villages and are still inaccessible to many a rural inhabitants as they are situated far away from many villages
- poor recovery of loan of RRBs: the average rate of recovery is around 55 per cent only
- most of the RRBs suffer from losses

- slow progress: many restrictions imposed by the sponsoring bank, NABARD, RBI and Government on RRBs operations are the causes for slow progress of them

POLICY SUGGESTIONS

- awareness for future planning: surplus income the rural poor people used to spend on social ceremonies and purchase of luxurious items mainly due to lack of awareness for proper future planning
- changing the mindset of people and encouragement to save are required
- rapid expansion of bank branches in all villages and doorstep delivery of services is required in the small villages as people do not have easy access to bank branches.
- these banks should try to connect the rural poor people through micro-credit and Self-Help Groups
- constant persuasion about the various savings schemes to the rural areas is required to enhance their saving habit.
- expansion of the insurance linked demand and time deposits should be offered by the RRBs to the rural poor people
- The multi-agency control over RRBs should be reduced
- Proper identification of beneficiaries for advances is essential
- Loans should be given only for productive purposes and to those projects which are able to generate sufficient surplus income for repayment
- For repayment of loans Recovery camps should be arranged at panchayat level in the harvesting season.

CONCLUSION

The economy of India is predominantly rural in character. Most of the rural people are suffering from the problem of poverty and unemployment. One of the main causes for these two problems is non-availability of finance.

The establishments of RRBs were essential to build up strong financial infrastructure for rural development. RRBs have been established under the RBI Act, 1976 which are functioning with a rural ethos and pro poor focus to develop the rural economy. Those banks provide loans and other facilities mostly to small and marginal farmers, landless agricultural labours, rural artisans, and rural small and cottage industries. RRBs have emerged as a state sponsored rural commercial banks.

This study exhibits considerable achievement of RRBs in expansion of rural credit to both the priority and non-priority sector. Although the banks face various challenges, yet a lot of opportunities still remain for their growth.

REFERENCES

- www.rbi.org.in
- www.nabard.org
- www.rrb.com
- Agrawal, Meenu, Role of RRBs in Economic Development, New century publications, New Delhi.
- Bhalla, G. S. and Gurmail Singh, 2009, "Economic Liberalization and Indian Agriculture:A State-wise Analysis," in *Economic and Political Weekly*, December 26.
- Chakrabarti, M., THE ROLE OF REGIONAL RURAL BANKs (RRBs) IN FINANCIAL INCLUSION: AN EMPIRICAL STUDY ON WEST BENGAL STATE IN INDIA, ABHINAV, VOLUME NO.2, ISSUE NO.8.
- Jain, M. K., ROLE OF REGIONAL RURAL BANKS IN THE DEVELOPEMENT OF INDIA, Global Journal of Multidiciplinary Studies,
- Ministry of rural development of India - http://rural.nic.in/sites/programmes-schemes.asp NABARD Annual Report various issues
- Naqi Uddin (2003)., *Regional Rural Banks and Development*, Mittal Publications, New Delhi.
- Prabha Sing, A. Kumar Singh and Amitkumar Varma, Economic and Social impact of RRBs, New century Publications, New Delhi- 2009.
- P. A. Steeven Raj, Merger and Amalgamation of RRBs, New century publications, New Delhi 2009.
- Ram, J.K., Regional Rural Banks of India: Evalution, Performance and Management Partridge Publishing India, 2015.
- Velayudham, T.K. and V Sankaranarayanan, 1990, '*Regional rural banks and rural credit: some issues* Economic and Political Weekly, September, 22.
- Venkatanaidu.G.(2012)., *Performance of Regional Rural Banks*, Southern Economist, October 15, 51 (12) PP. 9-12.

(Endnotes)

1 Jain, M. K., ROLE OF REGIONAL RURAL BANKS IN THE DEVELOPEMENT OF INDIA

2 Chakrabarti, M., THE ROLE OF REGIONAL RURAL BANKs (RRBs) IN FINANCIAL INCLUSION: AN EMPIRICAL STUDY ON WEST BENGAL STATE IN INDIA

3 Ram, J.K., Regional Rural Banks of India: Evalution, Performance and Management

2

Regional Rural Banks in India: Problems and Prospects

Santosh Koner
Jaydeb Sarkhel

INTRODUCTION

One of the points in the 20 point economic programme of Mrs. Indira Gandhi was liquidation of rural indebtedness and provision of institutional finance to farmers and artisans in rural areas. To fulfill this point regional rural banks (RRBs) were planned to be established. RRB Act was passed by the parliament in 1976 . Initially five RRBs were set up and then more and more RRBs came to be established throughout the country.

RRBs were set up on the recommendations of the Narasimham working group set up in 1973 which proposed the establishment of a new set of low cost banks for the rural poor. It was suggested that these banks would be a combination of cooperatives and commercial banks. Like the cooperatives they will feel and be familiar to the local problems and like the commercial banks they would have ability to mobilize deposits and access to central money markets.

Each RRB has three partners. The Govt. of India has 50% share, the sponsored commercial bank has 35% share and the concerned State Govt. has 15% share in the subscribed capital of the RRB.

OBJECTIVES

The objectives of the RRBs are as follows:-

- To mobilize savings in the form of deposits from the rural areas.
- To provide cheap and liberal credit facilities to the small and marginal farmers, agricultural labourers, artisans and small entrepreneurs.
- To spread banking habits among the rural people.
- To increase banking and financing facilities in backward and unbanked areas.
- To increase employment opportunities by encouraging trade and commerce in rural areas
- To encourage entrepreneurship in rural areas.
- To provide finance to cooperative societies, primary credit societies, agricultural marketing societies etc.
- To cater to the needs of the backward areas which are not covered by the other programmes of the government.
- To save the rural poor from the money lenders.
- To act as a catalyst in the economic development of the specified region by providing ancillary banking services.

RRBs are also commercial banks but they differ from commercial banks in certain respects:

First, commercial banks can operate in any region of the country subject to the permission of the RBI but an RRB can operate only in a specified region comprising one or more districts of a state.

Secondly, commercial banks can grant loan to any person approaching for loan and satisfying the criteria set by the banks for lending. The loan may be for productive purpose or for unproductive purpose. But RRBs can grant loans only to small and marginal farmers, rural artisans and agricultural labourers and others of small means for productive purposes only.

Thirdly, the commercial banks charge rates of interest determined by the market. But the lending rates of RRBs should not be higher than the prevailing lending rates of cooperative societies in any particular state.

Special facilities are given by the RBI and other institutions to RRBs so that they can manage competition from commercial banks.

- RRBs are allowed to maintain lower CRR and SLR than commercial banks.
- RRBs are allowed to pay 1/2% more interest on all deposits compared to the rates offered by commercial banks.
- Sponsor banks provide managerial and financial assistance to RRBs
- NABARD provides refinance facilities to RRBs. In fact NABARD is the regulatory authority for the RRBs.

ROLE OF RRBs

The role of RRBs cannot be ignored in the present day banking . They are working as alternative agencies to provide institutional credit in rural areas. In course of time they have almost reduced the position of village money lenders. The RRBs have been actively participating in programmes of poverty alleviation like SGSRY, PMRGY, IRDP, payment to anganwadi, old age pension, mid day meal, scholarship to students, Indira Awas Yojana, wage payment to MGNREGA beneficiaries etc. They are also implementing differential rate of interest(DRI) schemes for the weaker sections.

The RBI conducted a field survey in 1981 on all qualitative aspects of lending by RBBs. The findings of the study are as follows:

- RRBs have followed the instructions given by the RBI and the GOI regarding loan policies, procedures etc.
- The basic aim of setting up RRBs which is development of the rural economy by providing credit for the development of agriculture, trade, commerce, industry and other productive activities is being fulfilled.
- RRBs have successfully maintained their image as a small man's bank by confining their credit facilities to the target groups.
- The recovery position is not satisfactory.

In the words of the RBI study," The RRBs have fared well in achieving the objective of providing access to the weaker sections of the society to institutional credit but the recovery position on the whole is not satisfactory."

PROBLEMS OF RRBs

The Narasimham Committee-I on financial system(1991) evaluated the working of RRBs. According to this committee there were three basic problems:

> First, on account of several restrictions imposed on lending, RRBs could not earn higher incomes. For example they had to lend only to the target groups for productive purpose. They could not give loans to non-target groups and for consumption purposes. Moreover in most of the cases the rate of interest was low due to the DRI Scheme.
>
> Secondly, though planned as low cost banking, it could not be maintained. Initially the scales of pay of workers of RRBs were lower than the corresponding scales of pay of workers of commercial banks. But an award of a tribunal said that the scales would be similar in both the cases. This increase in costs also reduced the profitability of the RRBs.
>
> Thirdly, the sponsoring banks were also running their own branches in the area of operation of RRBs .This had increased competition and led to lower income for RRBs.

Apart from these three problems mentioned by Narasimham committee several other problems can also be mentioned.

1. Since people in rural areas have low incomes, they cannot save more. Hence RRBs cannot mobilize large deposits. They therefore, have to depend on NABARD for funds to give loans to the target groups.
2. There is lack of coordination between RRBs and other financial institutions like commercial banks, NABARD, and other cooperative banks. This adversely affects the working of these banks.
3. High overdue and poor recovery of loans are two problems faced by the RRBs. Accordingly the RRBs suffer from the problem of nonperforming assets(NPAs). This is also reflected in the capital adequacy norms. Most of the RRBs cannot satisfy the capital adequacy norm of having 9% CRAR.
4. RRBs suffer from inadequacy of staffs who are not properly trained. Loans are sanctioned without checking the credit worthiness of the borrowers. RRBs do not have a proper channel of recovery system.
5. In many cases new branches of RRBs have been opened not on the basis of sound business needs but on the basis of political pressure. The number of RRBs also went up due to the same reason. It has created a problem of regional imbalance in banking facilities provided by RRBs. The branches of RRBs are concentrated in some specific states and districts which already have branches of commercial banks.

The Narasimham Committee recommended that the commercial banks should form rural subsidiaries for their rural branches,. Each rural subsidiary should have a compact area of operation. The rural subsidiaries should be treated at par with RRBs in respect of CRR and SLR requirements and refinance facilities from NABARD. The RRBs may retain their identities or may be merged with the rural subsidiaries of their sponsor banks. If the RRBs decide to retain their identities, they should be permitted to engage in all types of banking business. Their focus should be on target groups but their lending should not be confined to target groups only.

The RBI appointed Bhandari Committee to recommend measures for restructuring RRBs. The Committee suggested some short term measures which have been introduced. These measures include the following:

I) RRBs were freed from their service area obligations.

II) They were allowed to increase their non target group financing.

III) They were permitted to relocate some of their nonviable loss making branches.

IV) They were given freedom to open extension counters.

V) They were given permission to grant loans for nonproductive purposes e.g. loans for the purchase of consumer durables.

VI) They were allowed to upgrade and deepen the range of their activities to cover non-fund based activities.

In spite of these measures some of the RRBs continued to suffer losses. Hence the GOI was forced to start the reform process for the RRBs. During a review carried out by the GOI in the year 2009 it was found that the CRAR of the RRBs was too low. Therefore K.C. Chakraborty Committee suggested bringing the CRAR of RRBs to at least 9% in a sustainable manner. The Committee recommended recapitalization support to the extent of Rs. 2200 crore to RRBs.

As several committees suggested for creation of viable RRBs by amalgamation of unviable RRBs, finally it was decided to amalgamate some of them on grounds of contiguity in a particular region. The process of amalgamation has continued till June, 2014 and out of the originally 196 RRBs , we have only 56 RRBs in July, 2014.

As per reports of June, 2014 the GOI has put on hold further amalgamation of RRBs. The GOI has conveyed to the sponsor banks that no fresh proposal of amalgamation should be taken up at present. At present the focus for RRBs will be on improving their performance including their profitability.

A Bill to amend the RRB Act is being considered by the parliamentary standing committee on finance. The amendments are aimed at increasing the pool of investors to tap capital for RRBs. Thus the GOI is exploring a new class of investors to raise capital for these banks. Government has been making various efforts to make RRBs profitable institutions by infusing fresh capital. The RRBs are allowed to lend to commercial projects, consortium finance, foreign currency, insurance business etc. RRBs are also fast moving towards core banking solution for effectiveness and to increase customer base.

We can end up our discussion by suggesting some measures which should be adopted to make the RRBs more viable.

1. Participation of the local people in the equity share capital of the RRBs should be allowed and encouraged.
2. Participation of the representative of the workers in the board of management of the RRBs should be permitted. This will improve industrial relations in the RRBs.
3. Local staff should be appointed as far as possible subject to fulfillment of usual norms for employment in banks.
4. The RRBs must strengthen effective credit administration by way of credit appraisal, monitoring the progress of loans and their efficient recovery.
5. The RRBs may relax their procedure for lending and make them easier and customer friendly for village borrowers.
6. Coordination between district level development planning and district level credit planning should be established in order to chart out the specific role of the RRBs as a development agency of the rural areas.
7. The Stae Government should also take keen interest in the growth and functioning of RRBs.
8. The RRBs may be permitted to lend up to 25% of their total advances to the richer section of the village society.
9. District level central cooperative banks may be allowed to sponsor with commercial banks in the setting up of RRBs. There would be close coordination between cooperative banks and RRBs.
10. The RRBs should prefer lending to groups rather than lending to individual borrowers. In the case of group lending the members of the group will be collectively responsible for repayment of loans as it happens in the case of self help groups. This will improve the recovery of loans of RRBs.

REFERENCES

1. Datt and Sundharam- Indian Economy, S.Chand & Co.
2. Sundharam and Varshney- Banking and financial system,. Sultan Chand and Sons.
3. Mithani and Gordon- Banking and Financial System, Himalaya publishing House.
4. Devi, N.S. " Problems and Prospects of Regional Rural Banks in India.", International Journal of Managerial Studies and Research, Vol-2, No-3, April, 2014, Page 69-72
5. Regional Rural banks- An overview at www. AIIBanking solutions. Com
6. Gupta, S.- "Rural Financing- Role of RRBS"- Kurukhetra, June, 2011
7. Velayudham and Sankaranarayanan- " Regional Rural Banks and Rural credit: Some Issues" Economic and Political Weekly, Sept. 22, 1990 Parg 2157-2164.

3

Measurement of Risks of Regional Rural Banks in India: An Alternative Approach

Debasish Sur
Dhanonjoy Kumar

INTRODUCTION

Risk Management is the process by which a bank identifies, measures, monitors and controls its risk exposure in order to ensure that risks are within the tolerance level set by the bank and are clearly understood at relevant levels across the bank. It is an essential task for every bank to mitigate instability in its earnings and to add value to its owners' wealth. So in today's challenging and competitive environment, the matter of designing suitable strategies for managing risks in accomplishing the wealth maximization objective of banks is of utmost importance. In running the business a bank is exposed to various risks from within or outside the organization. Nothing wrong with that, for risk-taking, is intrinsic to growth. Since risks and returns go hand in hand, banks cannot do away with the associated risks completely. Taking no risk may mean forgoing rewards. Risk management aims at ensuring that risk remains at an acceptable level or within an acceptable range. Therefore, for the achievement of entity objectives, banks should also manage risk to be within their risk appetites.

Regional Rural Banks (RRBs) have been in existence for around four decades in the Indian financial scene. They were configured as hybrid micro banking institutions, combining the local orientation and small scale lending culture of the cooperatives and the business culture of commercial banks. The principal objective of RRBs was to satisfy the credit needs of the relatively unserved sections in the rural areas, such as small and marginal farmers, agricultural labourers and socio-economically weaker people. In fact, the emergence of RRBs can be recognized as an attempt to enhance the efficacy of rural credit delivery mechanism in India. The RRBs have been playing a vital role in developing rural economy in India since their inception. A notable feature of their performance over the last four decades has been the massive expansion of their retail network in rural areas. However, the overall position of RRBs in India is not quite encouraging. The poor credit-deposit ratio is still making big dent on the desired functioning of RRBs (Pal & Sura, 2006). The paradigm shift of the Indian economy to a market-dominated open economic system in 1991 from a state-dominated subsidized financial system consequent upon the world wide wave in favour of globalization and liberalization gaining momentum in the last quarter of the twentieth century and signing of the Trade Related Intellectual Property Rights System (TRIPS) agreement in 1995 are considered as watershed events for the Indian industries in the recent time. With the spectacular changes in the milieu of banking practices in India due to significant changes in the business environment, the earning trends, cost behaviour pattern, operational strategies, credit policies, liquidity practices etc. The banking sectors have also changed considerably. Moreover some remarkable events took place in the last few years. The financial position of all RRBs was reviewed by the Chakraborty Committee in 2010 and the Committee recommended for recapitalization. Moreover, as per the recommendations of the Dr Vyas Committee, amalgamation process of RRBs started in 2013. As a result, there has been a drastic fall in the number of RRBs in India. It came down from 196 in 2013 to 56 in 2016.With these changes in the RRB sector in India; the patterns of various risks associated with the RRBs have witnessed notable changes. The RRBs had been forced to reorient their strategies for managing their risks in the post-reform era. Some of them have been able to adapt themselves to the new situation while others could not so reorient. In this backdrop, the present paper analyzes the different components of risk of RRBs, evaluates the various measures of such components and also suggests an alternative approach to the measurement of risks of RRBs.

The remainder of this paper is designed as follows. Section II narrates the different components of risk of RRBs. Section III is concerned with the measurement of risks of RRBs. Section IV deals with an alternative approach to risk measurement and Section V provides concluding remarks.

COMPONENTS OF RISK OF RRBS

Like other players in banking sector the RRBs are exposed to various risks from within or outside the banks. The total risk associated with a bank can broadly be divided into eight components, viz., credit risk, market risk, operational risk, liquidity risk, reputational risk, business risk, systematic risk and moral hazard. The first four are the major components of risk associated with the RRBs. The following paragraphs narrate the different components of risk in RRBs.

Credit Risk

A credit risk is the risk of default on a debt that may arise from a borrower failing to make required payments. In simple words, if a borrower fails to repay the loan taken from the bank because of inadequate income, loss in business, death, unwillingness or any other reasons, the bank faces credit risk. So the genesis of credit risk lies in instability in the bank's loan recovery capability.

Market Risk

Market risk is the risk of losses in on- or off-balance sheet positions that arise from movement in market prices. Market risk can also be divided into four categories: (i) Interest rate risk which stems from potential losses due to fluctuations in interest rate, (ii) Equity risk which arises out of potential losses due to fluctuations in stock price, (iii) Currency risk which emanates from potential losses due to international currency exchange rates and (iv) Commodity risk arising out of potential losses due to fluctuations in prices of agricultural, industrial and energy commodities. Generally, RRBs face interest rate risk and commodity risk.

Operational Risk

Operational risk is the risk associated with the operations of the bank. It can also be categorized as (i) Human risk arising out of potential losses due to a human error, done willingly or unconsciously, (ii) IT/System risk which emanates from potential losses due to system failures and programming errors, and (iii) Processes risk which stems from potential losses due to improper information processing, inaccuracy of data processing etc.

Liquidity Risk

Liquidity risk is the risk associated with the bank's ability to carry on day-to-day transactions. In other words, it is the risk associated with the bank's ability to meet unanticipated funds that are claimed by depositors. RRBs may face this kind of risk.

Reputational Risk

Reputational risk is the risk associated with the possibility of unpleasant happening due to loss of the bank's reputational capital. Just like any other bank or financial institution, a RRB faces reputational risk which may be triggered by the bank's activities, rumors about the bank, willing or unconscious non-compliance with regulations, data manipulation, bad customer service etc.

Business Risk

Business risk is the risk associated with dispersion of the expected operating profitability of a bank. It arises out of the failure of the bank's long term strategy, wrong forecasts of revenue, lack of flexibility and adaptability to market conditions etc.

Systematic Risk

Systemic risk is the risk which affects all the organizations belonging to the banking industry. It is associated with cascading failures where the failure of a significant player can cause the collapse of all the others in the industry.

Moral hazard

Moral hazard is the risk which arises if a significant player in the banking industry takes risks, knowing that any other player in the same industry else will have to face the burden of those risks. It generally occurs when the bank with more information about its actions or intentions has a tendency or incentive to behave inappropriately from the perspective of the banks with less information.

MEASUREMENT OF RISKS OF RRBS

There are several measures which can be used in ascertaining the values of different components o f risk. These measures can be broadly divided into two categories: (i) Non-statistical measures and (ii) Statistical measures.

A. Non-statistical Measures

Different components of risk of a RRB can be measured in various ways. The most common non-statistical measure is CAMELS approach.

CAMELS' model is a very popular comprehensive measure used in banking industry for the purpose of ascertaining the financial status of the banks. It also helps in anticipating the risk associated with the banks. While measuring financial status of the RRBs as well as risk associated with them, CAMELS model has been extensively used. The acronym 'CAMELS' stands for the following factors that are used in assessing the performance and risks of the RRBs:

Capital Adequacy (C)

Capital adequacy is an important element of the CAMELS model. It is the capital expected to maintain balance with the risks exposure of the bank such as credit risk, market risk and operational risk, in order to absorb the potential losses and protect the bank's debt holders (Dang, 2011). To achieve a high capital adequacy rating, the RRBs must comply with interest and dividend rules and practices. It is essential for a RRB to maintain depositors' confidence and preventing the bank from going bankrupt. Capital adequacy indicates the overall financial position of the banks and also the ability of the banks to meet their additional capital requirement. While analyzing capital adequacy of RRBs the following ratios can be used:

i) Capital Adequacy Ratio: It measures the capability of the RRBs to absorb their losses. The higher the ratio, the higher is the margin of protection to the depositors and the lower is the risk.

ii) Debt-Equity Ratio: It shows the proportion of external liability to owners' equity. The higher the ratio, the lower is the protection for the creditors and depositors and the greater is the risk.

iii) Advance to Assets Ratio: It indicates the bank's aggressiveness in lending which ultimately results in higher earning capability. The higher the ratio, the higher is the risk.

iv) Government Securities to Total Investment Ratio: It reflects the risk bearing capability of the RRBs. The higher the ratio, the lower is the risk associated with the bank.

Asset Quality (A)

Asset quality is also an integral component of the CAMELS model. It influences a RRB's earning capability. Poor asset quality is the major cause of most bank failures (Grier, 2007). The quality of assets is reflected by the efficiency of a bank's investment policies and practices. It is an important parameter to gauge the strength of bank. The prime objective of measuring the quality of assets is to examine the presence of non-performing assets

(NPAs) in the total assets. The following ratios can be applied in ascertaining asset quality:

i) Net NPAs to Total Assets Ratio: This ratio indicates the extent of NPAs in total assets of a RRB. It measures the credit risk associated with the bank. The higher the ratio, the higher is the credit risk.

ii) Net NPAs to Net Advances Ratio: It also indicates the percentage of NPAs in the net advances of a RRB. It shows the degree of credit risk associated with the RRB. The higher the ratio, the higher is the degree of credit risk associated with the bank.

iii) Total Investments to Total Assets Ratio: This ratio shows the extent of assets deployed in investment which, as per theoretical argument, does not form part of the core revenue of a RRB.

Management Efficiency (M)

Management efficiency is another important element of the CAMEL Model. It shows the capability of the management to identify measure and control risks of a RRB's day-to-day operations and to ensure the safe, sound, and efficient operation in compliance with applicable laws and regulations (Dang, 2011). As management efficiency is a qualitative aspect, its proper measurement a very hard task. Generally, the following ratios can be used in analyzing the management efficiency of the banks:

i) Advances to Deposits Ratio: It indicates the efficiency of the bank in managing the process followed in converting deposits into profitable advances. The higher the ratio, the higher is the management efficiency and lower is the risk associated with the bank.

ii) Business per Employee: It reflects the productivity of the bank's human resources. The higher the business per employee, the higher is the employees' efficiency and lower is the bank's risk.

iii) Net Earnings per Employee: It also indicates the efficiency of managing human resources of the banks. The higher the ratio, the higher is the efficiency and lower is the risk associated with the banks.

Earnings Quality (E)

Earning quality is a vital component of the CAMELS model. It discloses the bank's ability to get stable earnings. In fact, it measures the earning capability of the RRBs and also indicates the sustainability and growth in their future earnings. A consistent profit not only builds the public confidence in the bank but absorbs loan losses and provides sufficient provisions. It is also necessary for a balanced financial structure and helps in providing shareholders' reward. Thus consistently healthy earnings are essential to the sustainability of RRBs (Grier, 2007). While judging the earnings quality of the RRBs, the following ratios can be used:

i) Operating Profit to Working Fund Ratio: It shows the operating earning capability of the RRBs. The higher the ratio, the better is earnings quality and lower is the risk.

ii) Spread to Total Capital Employed Ratio: It also measures earnings quality of the RRBs. The difference between interest earned and interest expended is called Spread. The higher the ratio, the higher is the earning quality and lower is the risk associated with the bank.

iii) Interest Income to Total Revenue Ratio: It shows the income from lending operations as a percentage of the revenue generated by the RRB. The higher the ratio, the better is the quality of earnings and lower is the risk of the bank.

Liquidity (L)

Liquidity is also an important ingredient of the CAMELS model. There should be adequacy of liquidity sources compared to present and future needs, and availability of assets readily convertible to cash without undue loss. The fund management practices should ensure a RRB is able to maintain a level of liquidity sufficient to meet its financial obligations in a timely manner; and capable of quickly liquidating assets with minimal loss (Uniform Financial Institutions Rating System, 1997). RRBs have to take a proper care to hedge the liquidity risk; at the same time ensuring good percentage of funds are invested in high return generating securities, so that they are in a position to generate profit with provision of adequate liquidity to the depositors (Reddy & Prasad, 2011). For the purpose of assessing liquidity of the RRBs, the following ratios can be used:

i) Liquid Assets to Total Assets Ratio: It measures the liquidity of the RRBs. The higher the ratio, the liquidity of the bank and lower is its liquidity risk.

ii) Government Securities to Total Assets Ratio: It is also a liquidity indicator of the RRBs. The higher the ratio, the higher is the liquidity and lower is the risk.

iii) Liquid Assets to Total Deposits Ratio: It shows the availability of liquid resources to the bank depositors. The higher the ratio, the greater is the liquidity and lower is the risk of failing to meet depositors' claim.

iv) Loans to Total Deposits Ratio: This ratio discloses the extent in which deposits are kept for issuing loans and therefore, the bank's dependence in interbank markets. The lower this ratio , the better is the bank's liquidity status, while a value of less than one offers security for loans since deposits alone are sufficient to cover such loans (Christopoulos et. al. , 2011).

Sensitivity to Market Risk (S)

Sensitivity to market risk is another important element of the CAMELS model. It measures the extent to which potential changes in interest rates, foreign currency exchange rates, product purchase and selling prices affect the bank's profits and the value of its assets. Total securities to total assets ratio is a widely used measure of sensitivity to market risk. Market forces, especially in the last few years, consist of a major reason for changes in the viability of banks. Price movements in favour of a bank's portfolio may boost the Bank's results whereas unfavorable movements may create severe problems to the Bank. This ratio correlates a bank's total securities portfolio with its assets and discloses the percentage change of its portfolio in changes of interest rates or other issues related to the issuers of the securities. A low value of this ratio is better for the bank as it reflects that its sensitivity to market risk is appropriate while a higher value implies that the bank's portfolio is susceptible to market risk.

B. Statistical Measures

Among the various statistical approaches to measurement of risk as proposed by different experts in the field of finance, the 'coefficient of variation' of relevant ratios indicating different aspects of financial performance of RRBs became the most popular during the last four decades. According to this approach, the coefficients of variation of some widely used indicators of financial performance, such as credit to deposits ratio (CDR), capital adequacy ratio (CAR), non-performing asset ratio (NPAR), provision coverage ratio (PCR), return on assets ratio (ROAR) etc are ascertained in order to measure different components of risk of RRBs. The higher the value of the coefficient, the greater is the risk.

AN ALTERNATIVE APPROACH TO RRB RISK MEASUREMENT

Corrado Ginni, an Italian Statistician and Sociologist developed one model in 1912. It is popularly known as Ginni's coefficient. It is widely used in Social Sciences. For example, it is extensively used in Economics for the purpose of measuring inequality in income and wealth. Ginni's coefficient can use in measuring the values of different components of bank risk. Ginni's coefficient of mean difference is an absolute measure of dispersion and it is denoted by $\Delta 1$ while Ginni's coefficient of concentration is a relative measure of dispersion and it is denoted by G. Ginni's coefficient of mean difference ($\Delta 1$) is the ratio of g to m where g represents the sum total of the differences of the values of the observations, m is equal to n (n-1)/2 and g is the number of observations. Ginni's coefficient of concentration (G) is equal to $\Delta 1/2$ AM where AM is the arithmetic mean. It is well accepted that the relative measure of dispersion is a better measure as compared to its absolute one. So, G of different key ratios indicating financial performance of RRBs can be used at the time of ascertaining the values of various components of bank risk. G is a pure number and it is independent of units of measurement. It varies between + 1 and 0. If G is 0 then it indicates that there is no risk while if it is equal to +1 then it implies that the risk is maximum.

Ginni's coefficient has a theoretical appeal since it is based on all the values of the variable and the differences of values among themselves and not on deviations from some measures of central tendency. Traditionally, CV is used in measuring different component of risk. CV is a relative measure of dispersion. It represents the ratio of standard deviation (SD) to AM. SD is the 'root-mean-square deviations from mean'. So, while ascertaining the value of risk the deviations from AM are taken into consideration. But AM is a commonly used measure of central tendency which has certain severe shortcomings. First, AM is highly influenced by extremely high or low values. Recognizing the deviations from such measure of central tendency may, therefore, distort the value of risk. Secondly, in extremely asymmetrical distribution AM cannot be regarded as a suitable measure of central tendency. Thus, at the ascertaining risk if the distribution used is found skewed, the deviations from AM ascertained on such skewed distribution cannot reflect the true value of risk. Thirdly, in case of qualitative data, AM cannot be considered as a good measure of central tendency. In such case, only median can be recognized as the appropriate measure of central tendency. Risk is calculated using qualitative data. For example, CV of OPR or CV of OPCE is used in order to measure the degree of business risk. Similarly, CV of capital turnover ratio is used in ascertaining the value of capital productivity risk while liquidity risk can be computed by CV of current ratio or CV of quick ratio. So, the data relating to such ratios are qualitative in nature. The use of deviations from AM is not at all tenable in this case. However, Ginni's coefficient accounts for only the differences of values among themselves, the deviations from AM are not taken into consideration. Thus, Ginni's coefficient can be regarded as a better measure of risk as compared to the traditional one.

CONCLUDING REMARKS

Risk measurement is essential from the angle of bank management for certain reasons. If risk associated with a RRB is more or less accurately measured, the relative status of the bank within the given pattern of industry risk which reflects its capability to achieve stability can be assessed. Moreover, while making risk-return trade off measurement of risk is a must. Further, without proper measurement of different components of risk of RRBs it is next to impossible for the banks to make appropriate decisions relating to capital adequacy, liquidity policies, asset structure etc. But the conventional measures used for ascertaining risk as mentioned in finance literature possess severe limitations. In order to overcome such problems, Ginni's coefficient is suggested as an alternative approach to measurement of bank risk. This approach does not consider the deviations from such a measure of central tendency like AM which may fail to reflect the true value of risk. It recognizes only the differences of values among themselves while measuring the value of risk. Thus, the alternative approach proposed in this paper can be considered superior as compared to the traditional one.

REFERENCES

1. Christopoulos et. al. (2011). Could Lehman Brothers' Collapse Be Anticipated? An Examination Using CAMELS Rating System, *Internationa lBusiness Research,* Vol.4 No. 2, pp.11-19.
2. Dang, U.(2011). The CAMEL Rating Sustem in Banking Supervision, Published Thesis, International Businees Programme, Arcada University of Applied Sciences, *ARCADA*, pp.16-26.
3. Grier, Waymond A. (2007). *Credit Analysis of Financial Institutions*, 2nd ed., Euromoney Institution Investor PLC.
4. Pal, K. & Sura, J.S. (2006). *JIMS-8M, The Journal of Indian Management and Strategy*, Vol-11, No.4, pp. 4-12.
5. Reddy, D.M. & Prasad, K.V.M. (2011). Evaluating Performance of Regional Rural Banks: An Application of CAMEL Model, *Researchers World: Journal of Arts, Science & Commerce*, Vol. II, Issue 4, pp.61-67.
6. Uniform Financial Institutions Rating System (1997). *Statements of Policy*, The United States: Federal Deposit Insurance Corporation (FDIC).

4

Regional Rural Banks in Rural Economic Development of India : An Overview

Uttam Kumar Dutta

INTRODUCTION

Banking sector constitutes the core part of economic system. Indian economy is mainly agricultural economy and real India lies in villages. So village economy is the backbone of Indian economy. Without the development of the rural economy, the objectives of economic planning cannot be obtained. As per Indian Rural Development Report 2012-13 released in October 2013, rural India still battles with poverty and lack of basic infrastructure .

Certain important points of the report are:

- 30% population of the country lives Below Poverty Line (BPL).
- 80% of BPL population lives in rural areas.
- More than 40% of the rural poor belongs to scheduled castes and scheduled tribes.
- Maximum number of rural people lives in Jharkhand, Bihar, Assam, Orissa, Chhattisgarh, Uttar Pradesh and Madhya Pradesh.

The report highlighted that poverty concentrated in certain regions and social groups.

- More than 40% of rural people lacks electricity connections.
- 70% of rural households have no sanitation facilities.
- About 20% of rural families rely on non-farm employment as major source of their livelihood.
- 20% of rural people have none of the three basic services e.g. drinking water, sanitation and electricity.
- Income from farm livelihood are not sufficient for households.

About 70% of Indians depend on agriculture, 60% of industries are agro based, 50% of national income comes from rural sector and the agricultural sector is the largest foreign exchange earner to India.

With a view to ensuring sufficient flow of institutional credit for agriculture and other rural sectors Regional Rural Banks (RRBs) were established in 1975 as per recommendations of the Working Group under the chairmanship of Sri. M. Narashimham. RRBs were created to meet the excess demand for institutional credit in the local areas, particularly among the economically and socially marginalized sections. The RRBs mobilized financial resources from rural areas and grant loans and advances mostly to small and marginal farmers, agricultural labourers, rural artisans and small entrepreneurs. Subsequently, the RRBs were setup through the promulgation of RRB Act of 1976 . The RRBs Act 1976 succinctly sums up the overall vision to sub-serve both the developmental and the redistributive objectives. The first five RRBs are:

- Prathama Bank in Uttar Pradesh
- Gorakhpur Kshetriya Gramin Bank in Uttar Pradesh
- Haryana Krishi Gramin Bank in Harayana
- Gour Gramin Bank in West Bengal
- Jaipur –Nagpur Anchalik Gramin Bank , Rajasthan

In RRBs , there are three shareholders namely Government of India (50% share) , Sponsor Bank(35% share), and State Government (15% share). Therefore , RRBs are jointly owned by Government of India, Sponsor bank and respective State Governments. The important features of RRBs are:

- RRBs were mainly established to meet the credit requirement of small and marginal farmers , landless labourers, rural artisans, small entrepreneurs of rural India with a focus on agro sector.

- To penetrate and extend a helping hand in the growth process of the country
- To ensure sufficient flow of institutional credit in the rural areas for agricultural and other rural activities.

SPECIAL FACILITIES

RRBs enjoy certain special facilities to face competitions. These special facilities are given to RRBs by RBI and other institutions so that RRBs can manage competition from stronger banks like commercial banks. The special facilities are :

- RRBs are allowed to maintain a lower level of SLR than commercial banks.
- RRBs are permitted to pay half percent more interest on all deposits except those of 3 years and above.
- NABARD is the regulatory authority of RRBs. IDBI, NABARD, SIDBI and other Financial Institutions are statutorily required under the RRBs Act to provide financial and managerial support to RRBs.

SOME OPERATIONAL ACTIVITIES OF RRBs

a) Expansion of Branches:

In December 1975, the number of branches of RRBs was 17 and number of banks was 7 but upto March 1990 the total number of RRB branches was 14443 and the number of RRBs was 196. Naturally the number of RRB branches has significantly increased to provide rural credit and banking services to the rural people. During 2013-14 the RRBs opened 438 branches taking the cumulative number of branches to 19082 as on 31st March 2014 . The RRBs have been allocated 22000 villages and at places where opening of brick and morter branch is not considered viable the banks are allowed to start Ultra Small Branches (USBs) and thereafter a places where the USB reaches the desired level of business, the same can be upgraded into regular bank branches. The expansion of the number of RRBs branches can be depicted under Table I

Table I: Branches of RRBs in India
As on March 31st

YEAR	No. of RRBs branches
1990	14443
2010	15790
2011	16185
2012	16698
2013	17645
2014	19082

Source: Department of statistics and information management, RBI

b) Agricultural Credit Flow :

Table 2: Agricultural Credit flow at ground level (Rs Billion)

Institutions	2009-10	2010-11	2011-12	2012-13	2013-14
Commercial Banks	2858.00	3458.77	3686.16	4324.91	5214.96
Cooperative Banks	634.97	780.07	879.63	1112.03	1184.22
RRBs	352.17	442.93	544.50	636.81	833.07
Total	3845.14	4682.91	5110.29	6073.74	7232.25

Source Amrit Patel, Bank Credit to Agriculture Problems of Recovery and Non-Performing Assets, The Management Accountant, The Institute of Cost Accountants of India, January 2015, vol.50 no1 p.59

From Table 2 it is clear that RRBs are playing an important role in case of agricultural credit flow. During 2009-10 RRBs granted 9.15% of the total flow. In 2010-11, the percentage increased to 9.46. Again in 2011-12 , the percentage of flow increased to 10.65 . In 2012-13, the RRBs granted 10.48% of total credit offered by different institutions. In 2013-14, the percentage of agricultural credit flow granted by RRBs is 11.52. It is significantly increased in 2013-14. So it is obvious that the percentage of agricultural credit flow has been increased year after year.

c) Opening of no- frills accounts :

Basic banking no-frills account with zero or very low minimum balance and banking charges that make such accounts accessible to vast sections of the rural people. RRBs provide small overdraft in such accounts.

d) Achievement under PMJDY:

Pradhan Mantri Jan – Dhan Yojana (PMJDY) was started with a target to provide universal access to banking facilities starting with "Basic Saving Bank Account" with an overdraft upto Rs 5000 subject to satisfactory operation in the account for 6 months and Rupay Debit card with inbuilt accident insurance cover of Rs 1 lakh and providing social security schemes i.e., Pradhan Mantri Suraksha Bima Jojana , Pradhan Mantri Jeevan jyoti Bima Yojana and Atal Pension Yojana.

As on 20-04-2016 RRBs have opened 3.83 crore accounts under PMDJY with deposit of Rs 6480.21 crore. PMJDY scheme has not only found an entry in the Guinness Book of world records but along with Aadhaar Scheme has revolutionalised the method of providing subsidies to the rural people. At present through the Direct Benefit Transfer the government assistance to the poor and needy get directly credited to their bank accounts. This has not only ensured the benefit reaches the poor but also helped in plugging the leakages in the system.

e) Recovery Performance:

Table 3: Recovery as percentage to demand

Year	Recovery %
2009-10	80.1
2010-11	80.2
2011-12	81.6
2012-13	81.2
2013-14	81.9

Source Amrit Patel,op.cit,p.59

From Table 3 it is evident that there has been an improvement in the recovery percentage of direct agricultural advance during 2013-14. In 2009-10, the recovery percentage was 80.1 but it increased to 81.9% in 2013-14 . It indicates regarding the good efficiency of the management of RRBs.

f) Sector – wise loans issued by RRBs:

RRBs play an important role in the rural credit market. Loans given to the needy people are classified into 2 groups. One is priority sector and the other is non-priority sector. Priority sector consists of agriculture, small scale industry , small transport operators , small business housing , exports, education, professional micro finance through SHG etc. It has been observed that RRBs provide more percentage of loans to priority sector than non-priority sector. Since 2009-10 RRBs are providing more than 80% of total loans to the priority sector and gradually the percentage is increasing year after year.

g) Relaxation on KYC norms:

For opening bank accounts in case of small accounts the Know-Your- Customer (KYC) norms have been relaxed since August 2005. RRBs are now permitted to take any evidence as to the identity and address of the customer to their satisfaction. Naturally RRBs are getting more access to provide maximum amount of rural credit.

PROBLEMS FACED BY RRBs

Sometimes question arises why RRBs lost their focus . The main problems of RRBs are

a) Village politics :

The village politics also affected the RRBs . Soon the lending in rural areas was politicized and poor and needy farmers and other sections of rural India were ignored. Mounting losses are occuring due to non-viable level of operations in branches located at resource -poor areas.

b) Delay in decision making process:

RRBs are controlled by NABARD, RBI ,sponsoring banks, central government, state government etc. Naturally the decision making on certain important matters may be delayed. Recently the process has been simplified by passing the operational responsibility on to sponsor bank.

c) Problems regarding deposit mobilization :

Normally RRBs provide loans and advances to the rural people. They are not interested to serve the needs of the rich . Thus, RRBs are not able to attract the deposit from the potential sector.

d) Lack of co-ordination:

When we compare the progress of RRBs with other commercial banks, we find that the progress of RRBs is not upto the mark. Comparatively it is slow and one of the important reasons for this slow progressness is lack of co-ordination between RRBs and sponsoring banks.

e) Lack of training facilities :

Mainly the staff of RRBs is urban – oriented. They do not have sufficient knowledge regarding rural areas and this lack of knowledge sometimes may effect the performance and growth of RRBs . Inadequate skills in treasury management for profit orientation.

f) Lack of effective implementation of Performance Budgeting system:

RRBs have introduced Performance Budgeting System (PBS) but the there is a lack of giving due importance for its effective implementation. The budgeting system of the bank is primarily based upon the past performances of the branches. The business potentialities of the area which is an important constituent for such budgeting system is not being considered at the time of formulation of a branch budget.

SUGGESTIONS FOR IMPROVEMENT OF RRBs

a) To build confidence of the general public in the soundness of banking system that can motivate and encourage them to deposit their savings.

b) To reinforce the confidence of the lenders thereby increasing the flow of credit to large number of vulnerable and weaker sections of the society.

c) Government should encourage and support banks to take appropriate steps in rural development.

d) To reduce the cost of credit operations significantly by way of avoiding litigations.

e) RRBs must strengthen effective credit administration by way of credit appraisal, monitoring the progress of loans and their effective recovery.

f) To improve the operational efficiency of the staff and help them devote more time to develop new farmer - friendly savings, credit , insurance and payment products.

g) To expand the reaching of RRBs in the rural areas through alternate channels.

h) To augment loanable resources to accelerate the pace of farm growth and development.

i) The management of RRBs have to take certain important change in their investment policies , method of operations, opening of more branches, recovery system etc.

CONCLUSION

The establishment and expansion of RRBs no doubt play an important role for rural development. With the passage of four decades, the RRBs are now looked upon with hope for rejuvenating the rural India. Today RRBs are also providing the strongest banking network. There has been a tremendous achievement in disbursing loans and advances to both priority and non-priority sectors. So the government should take some effective remedial steps to make rural banking viable.

REFERENCES

- Anil Kumar Soni and Abhay Kapre, A study on current status of Regional Rural Banks in India, Abhinav , Journal of Research in Commerce and Management , www.abhinavjournal.com.vol.no2, Issue no.2 ISSN 2277-1166.
- Dr. M.Sayed Ibrahim, Role of Indian Regional Rural Banks(RRBs) The Priority sector Lending – An Analysis, International Management Journal , Vol.1 No.1-2 (January –December , 2012) pp25-32.
- Dr. Seema Rafique and Satish Manwani , Role of Regional Rural Banks(RRBs) in the Economic Development of India, International Journal of Advance Research in computer science and Management studies, ISSN:2321-7782(online) , vol.1, Issue 7, December 2013,pp.650-356.
- Dr. Amrit Patel , Bank credit to Agriculture Problems of Recovery and Non-Performing Assets , The Management Accountant, The Institute of Cost Accountants of India, Vol.50 No1, January 2015, pp.58-66.
- S.Mural ,Desruptive Innovation Indian Banking Industry , The Management Accountant , The Institute of Cost Accountants of India, vol51 No8, August 2016, pp63-70.
- Annual Reports of the Reserve Bank of India, Mumbai.

5

Regional Rural Banks and the Socio-Economic Development of India

Chittaranjan Sarkar

INTRODUCTION

The Regional Rural Banks (RRBs) are operating on a holistic approach to offer banking facilities among the rural people of India. Rural banking is very much significant to augment free access to banking for all keeping in view the fact that a majority of India's population still live in rural India for their sustenance. It is also to be mentioned here that regional disparities are persisting in full form all over the country even after its seventy years of independence and there are pockets where the lights of development have yet to reach for various reasons. Financial freedom in keeping money safe and spending as and when needed is very much accessible through the banking system. Over and above this, there is a buzzword of financial inclusion to reach banking facility at each and every corner of the society. Offering banking habits and providing banking facilities will have a definite bearing in developing the rural India by means of financial inclusion programmes. The regional rural banks can be the best intermediaries to work and maintain viable links among the people of rural India.

The RRBs in India were primarily established with the noble mission to supplement banking facilities in the unbanked areas with a focused approach to develop the rural economy by means of providing finance for the development of basic agriculture, trade, commerce, industry with an emphasis on rural and cottage industries. It was felt that there should be equal opportunities to the economically backward and socially marginalized people through the provisions of banking activities to help them overcome the impasse to their social mainframing at par with others in the society. RRBs have to be motivated and given autonomy to work especially in rural belts and concentrate their activities in rural hinterlands of the country for the socio-economic development of the common mass. Small and medium industries operating in rural areas should be provided with adequate bank financing for their expansion in business activities which in turn will magnify the employment opportunities, both direct and indirect employment, among the rural youths. Rural artisans, small entrepreneurs in cottage and handicrafts should be given financial assistance through RRBs to help them survive and grow amid all adversities. In order to provide access to low-cost banking facilities to the poor, the Narasimham Committee Report recommended for the establishment of a new set of bank to provide institutional support in the form of finance by combining the local feelings and sentiments to tap rural problems on a cooperative venture as may be possible with a commercial outlook both from the bank's angle and from the angle of the rural entrepreneurships.

Agriculture and rural sectors play an important role in India's overall development strategy in terms of income and employment generation and poverty alleviation. Great significance has, therefore, been accorded to develop appropriate institutions and mechanisms for catering to the credit requirements of these sectors. The Government of India promoted Regional Rural Banks (RRBs) through the RRBs Act of 1976 to bridge the gap in the flow of credit to the rural poor. The RRBs have a special place in the multi-agency approach adopted to provide agricultural and rural credit in India. These banks are state-sponsored, regionally-based and rural-oriented with capital investment support by the Central Government, respective State Government and the Lead Bank at 50%, 35% and 15% respectively.

Besides the RRBs, commercial and co-operative banks have also been catering to the credit requirements of the rural sector as a move towards the achievement of financial inclusion being the flagship programme of the Government of India. Financial Inclusion is an important priority of the Government. The objective of Financial Inclusion is to extend financial services to the large hitherto un-served population of the country to unlock its growth potential. To extend the reach of banking to those outside the formal banking system, Government and Reserve Bank of India (RBI) are taking various initiatives from time to time. Various policy initiatives have been taken from time to time in this respect by widening the bank branches of RRBs in rural areas as a focused attention along with other banks in the country.

SPREADING BRANCH NETWORK OF RRBs

Keeping in view the needs of opening more bank branches of RRBs so as to offer extensive banking facilities among the rural people, the number of branches of RRBs in India has increased from 19,082 as on 31st March, 2014 to 19,948 as on 31st March, 2015 registering an annual increase of 4.53 per cent in 2014-15 over the year 2013-14 by spreading the network of RRBs to 644 districts of India. All branches of RRBs are operating on CBS platform to cater to the needs of modern banking.

Table-1: Statement showing Bank Group and Population Group-wise number of functioning bank branches in India as on September 30, 2015

Bank Group	Rural	Semi-Urban	Urban	Metropolitan	Total
SBI & its Associates	7988	6700	4341	3689	22718
Nationalized Banks	21355 (43.62%)	16830 (48.25%)	12714 (54.28%)	11589 (54.84%)	62488 (48.67%)
Other Public Sector Banks	411	557	508	411	1887
Old Private Sector Banks	1417	2599	1469	1087	6572
New Private Sector Banks	3083	4290	3218	3869	14460
Foreign Banks	8	12	57	247	324
Regional Rural Banks	14696 (30.01%)	3895 (11.17%)	1116 (4.76%)	241 (1.14%)	19948 (15.53%)
India as a whole	48958	34883	23423	21133	128397

* Source: Annual Report, 2015-16, Ministry of Finance, Govt. of India

* Figures in parentheses show the percentage sharing of India as a whole by the regional rural banks and nationalized banks in India for the different bank groups spread over the country.

From Table-1 it is observed that out of total 48958 rural bank branches in India as on 30th September, 2015, 14696 bank branches (30.01%) represent regional rural bank branches and 21355 bank branches (43.62%) represent branches held by nationalized banks in India.

FINANCIAL PERFORMANCE OF RRBs

The RRBs are operating mostly in rural areas with a mission to provide finance to the rural people including farmers, local artisans, households etc. For carrying on the activities by the RRBs towards meeting financial needs of the rural people, the RRBs very often may have to depend on loan sanctioning on a most non-economic basis giving more emphasis on providing finance without thinking of getting the adequate return therefrom and this leads to non-recovery of loans and advances and creation of non-performing assets (NPAs). While scanning the financial performance of RRBs in India it may be highlighted that out of 56 RRBs, 51 have been able to improve their financial performance during 2014-15 recording a net profit of Rs.2744 crore as on 31st March, 2015 as against Rs.2694 crore in 2013-14, showing an annual growth of Rs. 50 crore amid stiff competition with other banks. However, 5 RRBs viz. Ellaquai Dehati Bank, Madhyanchal Gramin Bank, Nagaland Rural Bank, Odisha Gramya Bank and Utkal Grameen Bank have incurred losses to the tune of Rs.176 crore during the year 2014-15. The aggregate reserves of RRBs stood at Rs.18712 crore as on 31st March, 2015 as against Rs.15805 crore as on 31st March, 2014, while their net worth increased from Rs.22172 crore in 2013-14 to Rs.25083 crore during 2014-15.

ACCUMULATED LOSSES OF RRBs

The number of RRBs that had accumulated losses remained the same at 8 as on 31st March, 2015 as compared to previous year. However, the aggregate amount of accumulated loss of RRBs has increased from Rs.948 crore as on 31st March, 2014 to Rs.1072 crore as on as on 31st March, 2015 showing annual growth of 13.08% in 2014-15over 2013-14.

NON-PERFORMING ASSETS (NPA) OF RRBs

Non-performing asset (NPA) formation has been the traditional feature of banks making loans and advances to the common public and the business houses throughout India. Gross NPA of RRBs has increased from Rs.9708 crore as on 31st March, 2014 to Rs.10905 crore as on 31.3.2015. The gross NPA as a percentage has increased to 12.33% as on 31st March, 2015.

AGRICULTURAL CREDIT AND KISHAN CREDIT CARD (KCC) Scheme

Offering agricultural credit facilities to farmers on a reasonable and timely basis through banks is a prime need to boost agricultural production in the country. There is a succinct relationship between the availability of agricultural credit and the target agricultural production to accelerate the pace of socio-economic growth process. Keeping in view the needs of the farmers for agricultural credit, a target credit support is set for every year to be provided by the different Public Sector Banks, Private Sector Commercial Banks, RRBs and Cooperative Banks. As against the farm credit target of Rs.8,00,000 crore set for the year 2014-15, an amount of Rs. 8,45,328.23 crore was actually disbursed by the constituent banks during the year registering an excess credit support to the tune of Rs. 45,328.23 crore provided to the farmers.

The Kishan Credit Card (KKC) scheme which was introduced in India in 1998-99 is an innovative credit delivery system to provide timely credit support to marginal farmers to meet their agricultural needs for buying seeds, fertilizers, pesticides etc. for agricultural purposes. This scheme is being jointly shared by all Co-operative banks, RRBs and Public Sector Banks operating in India under the aegis of NABARD and RBI to promote a balanced growth in the country. As on 31st October, 2015 the number of total live and operative KCCs under the jurisdiction of Co-operative banks, RRBs and Public Sector Banks are 738 lakhs of which 388 lakhs have been issued by C-operative Banks, 125 lakhs by RRBs and 225 lakhs by Commercial Banks.

MERGERS OF RRBs

RRBs have been rendering their pivotal role in offering institutional credit support in rural areas, particularly to the agriculture sector. The RRBs suffer from various problems like lack of adequate finance, technological advancement etc. to combat with other banks operating in the country. RRBs, thus, are in need to adopt technology-based operations and capital upgradation for their growth and survival amid tight competitions. As a matter of the policy decision to make the RRBs more viable and competent, the Government of India has taken initiatives, in consultation with NABARD, the concerned State Government and sponsor banks, towards the process of merger and amalgamation of geographically contiguous RRBs in a state with the objective to minimize the cost of operation including overhead expenses and to optimize the use of technology-based banking operations. It is inherent that by means of merger and amalgamation, the capital base, area of operation, man-power and infrastructural set-up etc. will be strengthened by virtue of synergy impact. The deficiency of an RRB branch in one aspect may be replenished by the efficiency of another in that respect and vice-versa and by the process of their resource pooling through merger and amalgamation, the branches of RRBs in a specific geographical area will be much benefitted and they will be able to serve the far-flung areas of rural India in a better way and also more successfully. Up to 31st March, 2015, 44 RRBs have so far been amalgamated into 18 RRBs bringing down the number of RRBs to 56 from 82 to achieve the benefits of merger and amalgamation.

EMPHASIZING CSR ACTIVITIES THROUGH RRBs

The present ideology of mandatory CSR performance as per section 135 of the new Companies Act, 2013 by the corporate houses in areas like poverty eradication, extension of education among illiterate adults and other social activities etc. have become very much significant. The financial activities relating to such performances may be made ear-marked to be done only through RRBs having their wide banking network and good connectivity with the rural India. This will help a lot in running the banking activities by RRBs more fruitfully and purpose-oriented to serve the rural India and its people suffering from financial distress. The bank related financial activities for conducting the specific CSR performance like poverty eradication, extension of education among illiterate adults, providing safe drinking water in the community and other social activities etc. can be accomplished through the designated branches of RRBs spread over the country especially in the rural areas. This will in one hand help to increase the banking business of RRBs in rural areas so as to strengthen their operational activities and in other hand the local rural people will be benefitted much to avail financial support and other advantages from local branches of RRBs and will get the opportunity to enjoy banking habits for their safe and sustained livelihood.

CONCLUSION

The people of India are suffering from various adversities for their sustenance. Even after 70 years of attaining its independence from the British colonial power, India is more or less at the same stand point as it was in the pre-independence period with abject poverty and deprivation. A large portion of India's people still live in rural areas with primary agriculture and agricultural labourer as their basic means of livelihood in a most neglected and underprivileged manner. There is vivid social compartmentalization prevailing in the society in full form. Economic and social deprivations have ruined the base of India. Illiteracy, lack of infrastructural facilities and banking opportunities etc. have aggravated the situation. Extending banking services to rural mass for their development is very much needed to break the bottleneck of sustainable growth of rural India. The financing system followed by the banks should be made more liberal and rural-centric since finance plays its crucial role in social upliftment. The socio-economic decisions should be taken through the lens of the society and the rural people as far as possible keeping in view the fact that developing a nation becomes really fruitful only when it is taken for all and not for a specific section. Concentration of economic power in a few hands to the detriment of the common mass is a serious blunder to achieve socio-economic growth since it mars the spirit of development process. The Government, local authorities, NGOs and the distinguished public should come ahead to work together on a Public-Private-Partnership (PPP) model by extending their whole-hearted support and co-operation to build the country a real destination for each and everyone to live and prosper by arresting all forms of socio-economic deprivations.

REFERENCES:

1. Annual Report, 2015-16, Ministry of Finance, Govt. of India
2. www.nabard.org

6

Business Correspondent Agents of Banks in Rural Financial Inclusion: An Investigation in Sikkim After Demonetisation in India

Samirendra Nath Dhar
Pintu Prasad Jaiswal

THE GENESIS AND GROWTH OF BUSINESS CORRESPONDENTS OF BANKS

It was way back in February 2005 when the Hon'ble Finance Minister in the Union Budget 2005-06, expressed that the Government intends to continue with its effort to turn the focus of regional rural banks (RRBs), commercial banks, and cooperative banks towards providing credit, especially production credit, to rural households and farm households. The finance minister requested the Reserve Bank of India (RBI) to examine the issue of allowing banks to adopt the "agency model", by using the infrastructure of civil society organisations, rural kiosks and village knowledge centres, to provide credit support to rural and farm sectors .

The RBI then constituted an Internal Group to Examine Issues Relating to Rural Credit and Microfinance with Shri H. R. Khan, then Chief General Manager and Principal, College of Agricultural Banking (CAB), RBI, Pune as the Chairman. To deepen and widen the financial services provided by Regional Rural Banks and other banks, particularly to the under-serviced areas and the rural poor, the Group came up with two models, viz. the Business Facilitator Model and the Business Correspondent Model for providing non-financial support services and financial services as "pass through" agents respectively by using Micro Finance Institutions I/NGOs, Civil Society Organisations and other external entities.

Based on the recommendations of the above Internal Group, the Reserve Bank vide its circular DBOD.No.BL.BC.58/22.01.001/2005-06 dated January 25, 2006 permitted banks to utilise the services of these institutions and organisations (other than Non-Banking Financial Companies) as intermediaries in providing financial and banking services through the use of Business Facilitator (BF) and Business Correspondent (BC) models.

The BC model has been growing at an accelerating pace since November 2009 when the RBI advised banks to draw up a road map to establish presence in every village with a population above 2000 individuals, through the use of business correspondents and business facilitators. Apart from banking outlets, branchless banking connectivity had been extended to 5,34,477 villages by 31st March 2016, using banking correspondents, a sixteen-fold increase as compared to 31st March, 2010 (The Bharat Microfinance Report 2016). Banks have deployed more than 1.6 lakh Business Correspondent Agents/ Bank Mitras (BCAs/BMs) to provide banking services to unbanked households of the country under Pradhan Mantri Jan Dhan Yojana (PMJDY).

The system through which the BC model works is simple. A Bank appoints a BC Entity, which can be organizations registered as companies under section 25 of the Companies Act (example Fino Fintech Foundation, Samvriddhi Inclusive Growth Network (SIGN)) or societies like SEED Financial Services or NGOs. The BC entities have their technological partners like TCS, Integra Micro Systems (P) Ltd, etc. The BC entities appoint field workers or BCAs (Business Correspondent Agents) or BMs (Bank Mitras) to carry out the services and enlist them with their partner banks . In a deviation of this model certain banks appoint BC Agents directly without having the intermediation of BC Entities.

According to the guidelines (RBI 2006) the Business Correspondents can carry out services like (i) identification of borrowers and fitment of activities; (ii) collection and preliminary processing of loan applications including verification of primary information/data; (iii) creating awareness about savings and other products and education and advice on managing money and debt counselling; (iv) processing and submission of applications to banks; (v) promotion and nurturing Self Help Groups/ Joint Liability

Groups; (vi) post-sanction monitoring; (vii) monitoring and handholding of Self Help Groups/ Joint Liability Groups/ Credit Groups/ others; and (viii) follow-up for recovery. (ix) disbursal of small value credit, (x) recovery of principal / collection of interest (xi) collection of small value deposits (xii) sale of micro insurance/ mutual fund products/ pension products/ other third party products and (xiii) receipt and delivery of small value remittances/ other payment instruments.

From the above list it is quite evident that the aim of the BC model is to develop and sustain the association between unbanked populace and the formal financial system. The principal advantage lies in the fact that through Business Correspondents on the one hand banks get considerable reach to the rural population without physical presence in terms of branches while on the other people in rural and remote localities get easy access to basic banking facilities at their doorstep. Khan (2012) observes that BCs can bridge the gap between the service providers (the banks) and the service seekers (clients) who are under-served and unbanked; and this model has evolved to counter the scarcity of required manpower to reach all people in the current banking system. The model is considered unique because of its reach and scale, the quality of the services provided, and the technological platforms that have enabled these services (Kumar et al. 2006). The concept is however not new and has been successful in many countries including Brazil. "With close to 400,000 banking correspondents as of November 2013, Brazil has the largest agent network in the world. The number of banking correspondents in the country has grown exponentially over the past decade, while the number of bank branches has remained relatively constant. Brazil has largely overcome the distance barrier to financial access, and a majority of Brazilians—67% of the population—now pay at least one bill at an agent". However, success stories are not replete and several problems crop up while operating through this model. These need deliberations so as to sort out the thorns in the bed and ensure the desired goals.

GLITCHES AND HINDRANCES IN OPERATIONS OF THE BUSINESS CORRESPONDENT AGENTS

The characteristics of many programmes for social welfare through social banking and inclusion drives are that after formulation most of them are not tested for their viability and the hindrances that block the smooth running of these schemes. Usually after introduction of these schemes, there is a thrust from the government for rapid expansion and quick delivery so that time bound targets are achieved and can be exhibited as success milestones. In this race for quantitative targets, the qualitative aspects are not overlooked and the inherent problems in the systems of governance and delivery of inclusion schemes remain undetected or even ignored. The problems which occur at the micro level of the administration of the schemes are realized much later, usually when there is very little avenue for rectification and then the only way out is to withdraw these schemes or replace old wines in new bottles. The cases of IRDP (Integrated Rural Development Programme), MWS (Million Wells Schemes), SGSY (Swarnajayanti Gram Swarojgar Yojana) are illustrations of the aforesaid phenomena.

The BC model has been designed for financial inclusion by bringing the banker to the doorstep of clients is relatively new, but has ambitious targets ahead. Being a system where a network of bankers, BC entities and the individual BCAs and technology partners have to work in tandem, it is not often easy to ensure that all these parties work in perfect coordination for satisfactory service delivery.

Kaur and Sure (2013) found that BC agents authorized by an aggregator company are not functional even after 6-8 months because banks have not yet activated the user accounts. They also reported that existing customers are unable to transact due to various technical and connectivity issues which have to be resolved either by the bank or the BC company. This has lowered the transaction rate as well as customers' interest towards banking through agent outlets. Moreover The BC companies are unable to fix the technical issues as they are busy with expansion plans. At the same time, banks are not cooperative as they do not see high volumes of business through the BC channel.

The RBI working group (2009) under the chairmanship of Vijay Bhaskar examined the experience to date of the business correspondent (BC) model and reported that "as almost all BC transactions are cash based, the flow of cash with BCAs has been highlighted as the biggest issue. Besides the logistics of handling large volumes of cash, it leads to increased costs and added operational risks." The working group also reported that "beneficiaries of BC services are mostly illiterate and susceptible to misguidance. Further, at times, clients tend to perceive the BCs themselves as banks and not as functioning on behalf of the banks." The working group also commented on the earnings of the business correspondents and reported that "The commission paid by banks to the BCs is not considered adequate for a viable business model. There are costs involved in staff salaries, trainings, etc for which the current compensation structure is not generally adequate. A majority of BCs have reported losses and some of them have even suspended their operations."

CGAP report (2012) revealed that the existing regulations do not allow sufficient flexibility for the BC arrangement to be viable. It argued that most of the banks have not really encouraged and promoted the BC banking channel, as required. More pertinently, it observed that the majority of the no-frills accounts opened under this model were not operational.

FICCI's Report (2012) highlighted problems regarding the recruitment of BCs and reported that that although RBI permitted different categories of individuals to work as BCs, the number of BCs engaged are not adequate. Further highlighting the aspect of non-professionalism in BC entities the report states that they are mostly irregular in the maintenance of records and delay the processing of loans. The Grameen Foundation (2013) found that the BC model in India is far from attaining business viability or sustainability. Their investigations suggested that policies and regulations, lack of sufficient margins, varied motivations of the banks were the main reasons for the lag in the development of a sustainable BC model. The Nachiket Mor Committee on Comprehensive Financial Services for Small Businesses and Low Income Households (2013) reported that in March 2013, there were 2,21,341 business correspondents engaged by banks, having grown by 548 per cent since 2010. However, the fraction of them actively transacting was very low, particularly in rural areas and low-income urban neighbourhoods where they are most needed and alternate channels such as ATMs are not available. This has resulted in an absence of financial viability and several have now started to shut down.

The Bharat Microfinance Report (2016) highlighted several problems that have hindered the growth of the BC model. They include operational hurdles, such as cash handling, transporting, safekeeping, , irregular accounting, frauds, and misappropriations. Again, majority of no-frills accounts opened by BCs are inactive. This has raised concerns that the model may not be viable. As a result, there is a shortage of funding for building the capacity of BCs.

Similar problems have been noticed in the State of Sikkim and needs to be deliberated on and addressed. For this purpose micro level studies are necessary specially focusing on the individual business correspondents who work in the field.

BUSINESS CORRESPONDENT AGENTS IN SIKKIM – SOME CASES

Sikkim supports a network of over 100 BCs .Sikkim had formally launched its first Customer Service Point at the Village Perbing, East Sikkim sometime in the third week of January 2015. The State had aimed to set up 129 CSCs (Common Services Centre) as Business Correspondents of State Bank of India, Central Bank of India and United Bank of India before March 31, 2015. State Bank of India and Central Bank of India and United bank of India are the lead banks in the State. Out of 129 CSCs, 100 have already been set up. Some CSCs have already started BC Operation in East Sikkim by opening more than 200 accounts under Ranka SBI Branch East Sikkim. Training has been given to 15 VLEs in West & South Sikkim. The first batch of 35 VLEs from the State started operations as Business Correspondent of Central Bank of India on January 12, 2015.

These efforts for financial inclusion are laudable. However, the sustainability of such programmes do not only rest on increasing the number of BCs , but on assessing the operational practices and problems which form the key factors for success and sustainability of the financial inclusion drives. This paper therefore attempts to take up this task and examine the problems in some areas in the state of Sikkim by delving into specific cases of BCAs specially those who have been affected after demonetisation in India in November 2016. One of their key benefits of using cases is their ability to capture what Hodkinson and Hodkinson call 'lived reality'. As they put it, case studies have the potential, when applied successfully, to 'retain more of the "noise" of real life than many other types of research' (Hodkinson and Hodkinson, 2001). While attempting to study situations via cases it is natural that as one gains in depth of the study there is a loss in the breadth of the study. Moreover , cast in a narrative format, descriptive case studies can make complex situations accessible and interesting to a non-technical audience. Problems of BCAs are rather varied in nature and needs to be studied specifically in depth rather than resorting to broad aggregative analysis using quantitative methods. Three cases have been presented in this paper so as to give more of the noise of real life of BCAs. The information provided in the cases have been collected by direct interviews with the BCAs and on-site observations during their operations.

Case One

Samarjit Raha (name has been changed for confidentiality) is a BCA with the State Bank of India , Sombaria Branch in Soreng subdivision in Sikkim. Situated at an altitude of 3,700 feet, *Sombaria*, a small village is full of vegetation of temperate type and is located remotely in the extreme Western Sikkim. There are 425 households with a population of 2814 people in the Sub-Service Area of Sombaria, which comes under State Bank of India. He has been working as a BC Agent since last year (2015), though during the initial few month he did not receive any remuneration or commission, yet he continued working along with the link branch. He has a grocery shop, which provides an additional income to him. He was receiving a commission of Rs 12,000 per month on an average before demonetisation in India which has dropped to about Rs 7500 per month after demonetisation. However, Mr. Raha is not very satisfied with the commission being earned and operational hindrances and pointed out that:

- There is a lack of transparency in the computation of monthly commission, as they are not provided with a detailed break-up statement wherein the commission source is displayed. As per agreement between BC and Banks, 80% goes to BCAs and 20% to the BC & Sub-BC.(Since no Sub-BC exist currently in Sikkim, no one is aware about its collection and allocation).
- Mr. Raha can deal with SBI Tiny Account with Rs.50,000 as maximum balance ; while in April,2016 New SBI Tiny (Special) Account was offered where maximum balance is upto Rs.2,00,000 and Rs.20,000 per day per transaction is the maximum limit. However, after demonetization, customers can withdraw maximum Rs.2500 per day and can deposit money tuning to Rs.2500 per day (though during the initial 3 days there was a random collection of money) while the BC Agent are allowed to withdraw Rs.50,000 per day from the bank branch to serve their customer. still they are not provided adequately(he has received Rs.50,000 twice till date). As a result the Customer Service Points office is closed majority of days due to non-availability of the cash.
- Interoperability between banks has been completely stopped after demonetization due to which many other bank customers are not been able to transfer their money. Even though Micro-ATMs (Magstripe Card Reader and PIN pad) was supposed to be given to the BCAs/CSP operator, till date it has not been given to them.
- Since last five month there are no BC Co-ordinator and Sub-BC in Sikkim, leading towards chaotic situation. The BCAs feel that their business can develop and revenue may increase if local person is hired as a BC Coordinator.
- Banks do not recognize BC Agents as their partner in mobilizing revenue instead they treat them at par with customer asking them to stand in queue along with other customer, in addition managers are also unaware about their functioning and systems.
- Earlier VSAT was assured to be given to them in the BC Agent meeting, wherever a weaker network was hindering the services. Nothing has been done so far in Sikkim. There is a similar situation ith POS machines. After repeated demands by many CSP operators only few of them could get it.

- Even though the Account is opened by the BCAs, the passbook is given to the customer by the bank at the branches. After demonetization, it is being found that account numbers are not being generated quickly even after uploading the account opening information, which is leading towards hassles to the poor people with low literacy as they cannot recall their account numbers.
- While opening an account a left finger impression is captured and is required for doing a transaction at CSP. There has been a case where the same finger print mark of the customer is not accepted by the biometric device leading towards a failure in transaction. The BCAs do not have the right to change the finger print capture as it can be done only from the Link Branch Manager Computer, but it has been observed that they too take lot of time to update it, leading towards more harassment both to the BCA and Customer.

Case Two

Ramesh Bhattarai (name has been changed for confidentiality) works as a BCA in Samdong Kambal , a village in Rakdong Tintek Tehsil in East District of Sikkim. It is located 27 KM towards south from district head quarters in Gangtok. His bank branch is SBI, Dikchu. He has been working as a BCA since 2015 with a fixed monthly incentive of Rs.2000 pm for which at least 20 accounts has to be opened. His earnings from commissions as BCA was Rs 5000 in August 2016, Rs 6200 in September 2016, Rs 9000 in October 2016. His earnings from commissions crashed to Rs 4,100 after the announcement of demonetisation in November 2016. Ramesh expressed the following glitches that hindered his operations as a BCA:

- BCAs are required to have a settlement account with the link branch wherein they have to maintain a sufficient balance ranging from Rs.50,000 to Rs.1,00,000. This amounts are blocked in the BCs operation throughout the year and the commission they earn varies from Rs.3,000 to Rs.10,000. They feel that they are not earning substantial earning from this capital and every time they are low with the balance are required to visit the link branch incurring additional expenses just to deposit the money. Many of them feel that they should be provided overdraft facilities from the branch. Even MGNREGA worker earns more than the BCAs in a number of cases which is demoralizing to continue with the BC operation.
- BCAs are not allowed to process the loan application in the link branch, neither any small value credit can be disbursed, nor mutual fund products or third party products can be sold by them. Unofficially, BCAs are asked to process Mudra loan, mutual fund producst, Sukanya Samriddhi, etc by the link branch wherein no commission is guaranteed. They feel their business can grow if they can deal with these producst officially with commission.

- Initially CSP were assured Rs.5000 per month as fixed incentives but till date they are receiving Rs.2000 pm only as a fixed incentive. Though they have conveyed many times that it is tough to operate due to a sparse population and difficult terrain still no measures are taken for them.
- Many of the BCAs feel that they should be trained continuously and the awareness camp should be undertaken to make common people aware about the usage of banking product and services. Now when the government is talking about digital and cashless economy, the backward section should be taken care of if the objective is to be achieved. Initiatives are rarely being taken in the field. Even the bank officials do not visit the CSP regularly and no such public awareness camp is organized.
- BCAs are not given any special preference in the link branches which again create a negative perception about them in the mind of common people, when they see them in the queue along with them.
- After demonetization, BCAs are hardly hit as they are not in a position to supply cash to the customer. Even though RBI issued a guideline to supply Rs.50000 per day to the BCAs still the banks are unable to comply with it. Many of the BCAs have shut their office citing the cash crunch as customer face-off occurs frequently. The BCs customer ask their money back and when they are requested to visit the link branch, they do not get their money which sometime lead towards a heated argument with the BCAs.
- Currently only Rs.2500 is accepted as deposit and withdrawal per day from the BCs customer account which has completely reduced the transaction volume as well as commission. Immediately after demonetization, IMPS or interoperability service was closed and for the first two week only kiosk account opened by BCAs at their CSP were functional. Later on AEPS (Adhaar Enabled Payment System- SBI account of other branch) transaction was enabled.

Case Three

Sunil Chettri (name has been changed for confidentiality) has been working as a BCA for Central Bank of India , Renok in Sikkim. His area of operation is in Sudunglakha (sub-divison – Rongli) . There are 1775 people in the Sub-Service Area of Sudunglakha, which comes under Central Bank of India Renock branch. Sudunglakha is a Village in Rhenock Tehsil in East District District of Sikkim State, India. It is located 54 KM towards South from District head quarters Gangtok. 3 KM from Rhenock Tarpin. The total geographical area of village is 258.09 hectares and there are about 206 houses in Sudunglakha village. Rangpo is nearest town to Sudunglakha which is approximately 28km away. He is working as a BC Agent since last year (2015). Interviews with him brought out the following

- The BCAs of Central Bank of India are functioning in a situation wherein no monthly fixed incentives is provided to them, though it was agreed at the initial stage and the only source of income being commission which is again on transaction basis. Sunil earned Rs 900 in August 2016, Rs 1220 in September, Rs 1980 in October which declined to Rs 1200 in November. Demonetisation has had its after effects and the cash strapped families have literally been forced to desist from making any financial transaction. Loan disbursals have had to be discontinued as the link bank could not provide the required supply of cash.
- BCAs are completely frustrated as there are no fixed incentive and their earning are even less than MGNREGA workers. It has been observed that many of them are charging extra commission for each transaction to sustain (though officially they do not accept it), which is again adding additional burden on the customer (as the cost of travelling to the bank is high). They are continuing the operation due to a good relation and image develops in the village and expecting that the situation will be better in the near future.
- BCAs of CBI can only offer services to the CBI customer, interoperability services has not been activated till now, which is again curtailing their income source and adding problem to the customer. POS machine has been provided to few of them who can serve only the home bank customer.
- There are no grievance redressal mechanisms available for the customer. Even if they approach the bank branch they are ask to contact the concerned BCAs for r redress..
- The only product available to them is a tiny deposit account. The maximum deposit and withdrawal before demonetization was Rs.10,000 per day. After demonetization they are not being able to serve their customer due to a non-availability of the cash from the branch, thus adding financial burden to a poor people who are forced to travel a distance sacrificing their daily wages just to withdraw their own hard earn money.
- The major drawback in their functioning is the lack of BC Coordinator and Sub-BC presence as there is no one in the system to address their concern even though 20% of the total commission being earned is deducted as a share of BC and Sub-BC.

CONCLUSIONS

The cases presented above are indicative and not exhaustive. However, as experienced and observed by the researchers, the conditions of many more BCAs are quite the same. The conditions of the BCs are similar to what had been identified by the Nachiket Mor Committee of RBI (2013). BC Agents had joined the financial inclusion drive with lot of expectations, but the hindrances being faced by them are diluting their expectations . Monetary benefits derived from commissions remain to be low and irregular, and show indications of dropping down further due to cash crisis after demonetisation. Steps have to be taken for ensuring regularity of income and adequate income to BC agents. This can be done by a combination of three policies: (i) enhancing the commission rate per transaction (ii) increasing the number of transactions, which is possible by enhancing the technological aspects of operations and (iii) prompt disclosure and documentation of remuneration rates and process of computation of commission on account of transactions and NPA recovery. Moreover the BCAs need to diversify to sale of micro insurance products, mutual fund products and micro pension products instead of restricting their activities to mere handling of small deposits and loans.

The prospects of a cashless environment are a remote possibility since the connectivity problems of the POS machines are difficult to address in these remote villages. The link banks therefore need to ensure adequate cash flow to the BCAs and treat them with priority so that cash withdrawal and deposit activities are faster. Again without adequate financial literacy and lack of awareness, the rural customers do not always venture to transact with the BCAs and hence transaction volumes remain low. Increasing awareness of beneficiaries about long term financial inclusion benefits and bringing to their knowledge how this can be achieved through frequent interaction with the BC field workers has to be initiated by the link banks. The beneficiaries have to be made aware of the fact that it is not enough to just open a basic savings bank deposit(BSBD) account under financial inclusion schemes such as Jan-Dhan but keep the accounts active through regular transactions. Such regular transactions can be ensured only if the rural folk are included in viable livelihood schemes through NRLM (National Rural Livelihood Mission). Banks should conduct awareness camps so that the rural people comprehend and appreciate of the BC model . The BC model has been designed for attaining 100% financial inclusion and it has to ensured that BSBD accounts are actually accessed and utilised for the purposes for which they are designed . The possibility of wrong utilization of these accounts for parking unaccounted money by others specially during demonetisation drives gets reduced.

REFERENCES

1. CGAP (Consultative Group to Assist the Poor) (2012). *Business Correspondents and Facilitators: Pathway to Financial Inclusion?* , Access Development Service, New Delhi.

2. FICCI (Federation of Indian Commerce and Industry) (2012). "*Promoting Financial Inclusion: Can the constraints of political economy be overcome?*", FICCI Federation House, New Delhi.

3. Grameen Foundation USA and Enclude (2013), *Discussion Paper s On India's Business Correspondent Model And the Operational challenges faced by BCs in the field* .

4. Hodkinson, P. and H. Hodkinson (2001). The Strengths and Limitations of Case Study Research. Paper presented to the Learning and Skills Development Agency conference, *Making an Impact on Policy and Practice,* Cambridge, 5-7 December 2001, downloaded from http://education.exeter.ac.uk/tlc/docs/publications/LE_PH_PUB_05.12.01.rtf.26.01.2013.

5. Kaur1.S., and Y. Sure (2013). Business innovations in Indian banks for Financial Inclusion *IOSR Journal of Business and Management (IOSR-JBM)* e-ISSN: 2278-487X, p-ISSN: 2319-7668 PP 71-77 www.iosrjournals.org.

6. Khan, R. Harun.(2012), "Issues and Challenges in Financial Inclusion: Policies, Partnerships, Processes and Products", *RBI Monthly Bulletin,* , pp.1447-57.

7. Kumar, A., Nair, A., Parsons, A., and Urdapilleta, E. Expanding bank outreach through retail partnerships: Correspondent banking in Brazil. *World Bank Working Paper 85,* Washington, DC, 2006.

8. RBI (2013), *Report on Comprehensive Financial Services for Small Businesses and Low Income Households* under the chairmanship of Dr. Nachiket Mor.

9. RBI (2009) *Report of the Working Group to Review the Business Correspondent Model* under chairmanship of P. Vijaya Bhaskar August 18.

10. RBI (2006) RBI Circular no RBI/2005-06/288 DBOD.No.BL.BC. 58/22.01.001/2005-2006 dated Jan 25, 2006.

11. The Bharat Microfinance Report (2016), Sa-Dhan, The Association of Community Development Finance Institutions.

7

Financial Inclusion through Regional Rural Banks in India: An Empirical Assessment

Krishna Singh

INTRODUCTION

In India Regional Rural Banks (RRBs) came into existence on 26th September 1975 with the objective of satisfying credit needs of relatively deprived sections in rural area, such as small farmers, agricultural labourers and socio-economically weaker people. Gandhiji says "Real India lies in the villages". The genesis of the rationale for establishing RRBs in India lies in the statement made by our great leader. The share capital of RRB was contributed by Government of India, the concerned State Government and the sponsored bank in the proportion of 50%, 15% and 35%, respectively. RRBs also provide loans and advances mostly to farmers, rural and artisans as well as to the lower sector of the society.

The dynamics of development in a growing economy involves the improvement in the provision of financial facilities or services even at the doorstep of the most downtrodden sections of the economy. This is because in terms of modern views of development, peoples' livelihood opportunities are conditioned by capability generation that leads to access to asset base which is productive of income. However, it is ultimately the aspect of financial inclusion which involves the delivery of financial facilities at an affordable cost to the vast sections of disadvantaged and low income groups.

Broadly speaking, financial inclusion means extending access to finance and financial services to all in a fair, transparent and equitable manner at an affordable cost (Sarma, 2008; Solo, 2008).The Government of India's 'Committee on Financial Inclusion in India' defines financial inclusion 'as the process of ensuring access to financial services and timely adequate credit where needed by vulnerable groups such as the weaker sections and low income groups at an affordable cost' (Rangarajan Committee, 2008).

The importance of financial inclusion is felt mostly in the context of a vast chunk of poor people in India who remain deprived of adequate access to needed financial facilities. According to Morduch and Rutherford(2003), this marginalized group of people feels a great need for financial facilities which should be flexible, reliable, continuous, easily operable and sensible to their requirements. RRBs have the potentiality to play an important role in financial inclusion primarily because of their geographical location in remote places in the country. The objective of financial inclusion would be fully achieved if RRBs are able to bring banking to the doorstep of the customers.

The present paper is structured as follows. Section 2 presents the review of related literature and identifies the research gap. Section 3 states the objectives of the study. The data source is mentioned in Section 4. Section 5 narrates the methodology adopted in the study and also discusses the theoretical framework. Subsection 5.1 is devoted to analyze the development of a financial inclusion index. Section 6 deals with the analysis of the major findings derived from the study. Subsection 6.1 is concerned with an overall analysis of RRBs in India while subsection 6.2 focuses on the performance of the states in respect of financial inclusion index. Finally in section 7 concluding observations are presented.

REVIEW OF LITERATURE

The review of some significant studies relating to the issue addressed in the present paper which have been made in India in the recent past is narrated below:

Pathak and Raees (2015) carried out a study in which the extent of financial inclusion through RRBs in India was analyzed. The study revealed that RRBs made a notable contribution towards the development of the backward section of the society through financial inclusion. The study also observed that the spread of financial inclusion in India through RRBs was more than significant.

The study conducted by Ahmed (2015) assessed the performance of RRBs in India with respect to deposit mobilization, credit channelization, and credit to deposit ratio. The study showed that the reform measures had a positive impact on mobilization of the rural deposits as reflected in the increase in deposit per branch of RRBs. The study revealed that along with the increase of deposits, loans and advances increased at the same proportion.

Reddy and Prasad (2011) in their study examined the performance of the RRBs in India. The study revealed that the RRBs penetrated every corner of the country and extended a helping hand in the growth of the economy. Another significant outcome of the study was that despite the fact that RRBs, for over three decades, achieved performance to the expected level quantitatively, they had not turned towards sound financial management and productivity.

Rao and Rao (2016) in their study examined the performance of RRBs in respect of financial inclusion. The study found an interesting trend. The study revealed that although RRBs had the ability to mobilize small savings of the rural sector, they were relatively less successful in enhancing the flow of credit to the targeted rural poor. The researchers also argued that in order to survive effectively, the RRBs should have adequate technology to provide efficient service to their customers.

A large number of studies on the RRBs have been carried out in India during the last few decades. A considerable number of studies on this issue associated with RRBs have also been conducted in India. The RRBs in India have been playing a vital role in the financial inclusion. But no significant study on the aspect of financial inclusion index related to RRBs has so far been made applying principal component method. In order to bridge the gap the present study was conducted.

OBJECTIVES OF THE STUDY

The study has the following objectives:

(i) To assess the performance of RRBs in India over the study period.

(ii) To develop a financial inclusion index through application of principal component method.

(iii) To analyze the observed financial inclusion scenario across the states in India.

SOURCE OF DATA

The study is completely based on secondary data. It covers 21 major states in India during the period 2001 to 2015. While constructing the financial inclusion index (FII), three dimensions, namely branch penetration (BP), deposit penetration (DP), and credit penetration (CP) have been considered. The BPhas been measured in this study by number of branches, DP has been ascertained by amount of deposit in RRBs and CP has been measured by credit generated through RRBs. All these indicators have been taken from Reserve bank of India website.

METHODOLOGY OF THE STUDY

In this study Principal Component Analysis (PCA) has been applied in ascertaining financial inclusion index. Principal component analysis is a statistical procedure that uses an orthogonal transformation to convert a set of observations of possibly correlated variables into a set of values of linearly uncorrelated variables. The relevance of this method lies in the fact that it transforms the impact of a rather greater number of variables (which may be correlated) into a smaller set of uncorrelated factors. The number of principal components is less than or equal to the number of original variables. Since a number of indicators are involved in each category of inclusion or empowerment, use of PCA appears to be most appropriate index in order to derive a single index reflective of overall inclusion. A primary benefit of PCA arises from quantifying the importance of each dimension for describing the variability of a data set (Shlens, 2009). PCA can also be used to compress the data by reducing the number of dimensions without much loss of information. When using principal component analysis to analyze a data set, it is usually possible to explain a large percentage of the total variance with only a few components. Principal components are selected so that each successive one explains a maximum of the remaining variance.

Development of a Financial Inclusion Index

There are large variations across state specific values of the different indicators of financial inclusion. In order to ensure better comparability of these data, each indicator has been "normalized" using the UNDP goal-post method as used for measuring the initial international HDI. This is as follows:

$$X_i = \frac{(x_i - x_{mim})}{(x_{max} - x_{mim})}$$

Where Xi is the normalized indicator for state *i*, x_i is the corresponding pre-normalization figure, and x_{max} and x_{mim} are the maximum and minimum values of the same indicator across all the states. The normalized indicator takes a value 0 representing the lower end of the state's scale of financial inclusion while1 indicates the top end of the state's degree of inclusion for all the individual categories of indicators, and which varies between 0 and 1 for all other states. Based on the aforesaid normalized figures, principal component analysis has been applied in measuring the state specific financial inclusion index.

Credit Rating Information Services of India Limited (CRISIL) measures the financial inclusion in the form of an index. Three basic parameters of financial service, such as branch penetration, deposit penetration, and credit penetration are considered at the time of constructing the index. Here these three types of penetration have been ascertained by the indicators like number of branches, amount of deposit and amount of credit generated respectively.

Preparing a financial inclusion index on the basis of principal component method requires the consideration of diverse individual categories of financial services. The financial index is considered as a latent or unobserved variable. Here the problem is the weight assignment to the individual indicators which is critical to maximize the information from a data set included in an index. A good composite index should comprise important information from all the indicators, but not strongly biased towards one or more of these indicators.

The financial inclusion index linearly determined by three relevant components has been considered. The indicators are numbers of bank branches, amount of deposits in the RRBs and amount of credit generated. In latent form the financial inclusion index (FII)can be expressed as

$$(FII)_i = \alpha_1 (BR)_i + \alpha_2 (DEP)_i + \alpha_3 (CR)_i$$

$\lambda_j^{'} = 1, 2, 3)$ is denoted as the jthEigen value. Subscript j refers to the number of principal components that also coincides with the number of corresponding indicators. The values of $P_j^{'}$ gradually falls as the suffix increases, (j = 1, 2, 3) is denoted as the jth principal component. The corresponding inclusion index is obtained according to the following weighted average:

$$FII = \frac{\sum_{j=1}^{3} \lambda_j^{'} P_j^{'}}{\sum_{j=1}^{3} \lambda_j^{'}}$$

RESULTS AND DISCUSSION

Performance of Regional Rural Banks in India

Table 1reveals that in India number of branches, generation of credit and deposit per branch haveincreased during the study period.

Table-1: Overview of Regional Rural Banks in India

Year	Number of Branches	Amount of Credit Per Branch (Crore)	Amount of Deposit Per Branch (Crore)	Credit-Deposit Ratio (%)
2001	14431	1.088	2.619	41.6
2002	14486	1.284	3.058	41.9
2003	14462	1.528	3.444	44.4
2004	14484	1.802	3.853	46.8
2005	14433	2.259	4.254	53.0
2006	14372	2.741	4.912	55.9
2007	14422	3.342	5.693	58.7
2008	14558	4.025	6.684	60.2
2009	15010	4.470	7.908	56.5
2010	15303	5.456	9.305	58.6
2011	15658	6.272	10.467	59.9
2012	16170	7.211	11.317	63.7
2013	16985	8.048	12.158	66.2
2014	17901	8.882	13.038	68.1
2015	19472	9.306	13.671	68.1

Source: Authors calculation from secondary data

It is observed from the Table 1 that the amount of deposit per branch has increased from Rs. 2.61 crore to Rs. 13.67 core in the year 2015. The generation of credit per branch has also increased to Rs. 9.306 crore in 2015 from Rs. 1.08 in 2001. This table also shows that the growth rate of credit and deposit per branch has stepped up at a higher rate compared to the growth rate of number of branches. It implies that branches have become efficient to generate credit and deposit over time.

The credit to deposit ratio is one of the indicators used in measuring the efficiency of a bank's participation in the developmental process. Table 1 also discloses that the credit to deposit ratio of the RRBs has increased over the years under study. The ratio has increased to 68.1 per cent in 2015 from 41.6 percent in the year 2001.

Performance of the states with respect to Financial Inclusion Index

Table 2 depicts the relative position of the states in terms of financial inclusion through RRBs. A wide variation in financial inclusion index across the selected states over the years under study has been noticed. The higher the value of the index, the better is the performance of the states with regard to financial services.

Table-2: Financial Inclusion Index across the States

States	2001	2002	2003	2004	2005	2006	2007	2007	2008
Haryana	0.157	0.170	0.153	0.169	0.165	0.175	0.197	0.209	0.223
Himachal Pradesh	0.014	0.019	0.018	0.013	0.013	0.010	0.010	0.012	0.010
Jammu and Kashmir	0.045	0.048	0.047	0.046	0.048	0.040	0.038	0.037	0.035
Punjab	0.053	0.073	0.051	0.061	0.068	0.062	0.060	0.074	0.087
Rajasthan	0.456	0.478	0.478	0.487	0.495	0.497	0.507	0.529	0.539
Assam	0.110	0.155	0.148	0.155	0.164	0.146	0.153	0.153	0.151
Tripura	0.000	0.005	0.000	0.000	0.018	0.012	0.020	0.008	0.016
Bihar	0.602	0.608	0.612	0.633	0.622	0.616	0.641	0.661	0.683
Jharkhand	0.134	0.130	0.111	0.120	0.128	0.122	0.113	0.110	0.105
Orissa	0.386	0.430	0.417	0.440	0.436	0.417	0.421	0.422	0.422
West Bengal	0.453	0.477	0.463	0.463	0.451	0.436	0.418	0.412	0.402
Chhattisgarh	0.111	0.139	0.131	0.130	0.137	0.130	0.134	0.132	0.135
Madhya Pradesh	0.480	0.494	0.489	0.507	0.504	0.503	0.522	0.522	0.516
Uttar Pradesh	1.617	1.619	1.638	1.647	1.640	1.645	1.647	1.647	1.655
Uttarakhand	0.017	0.035	0.017	0.017	0.015	0.016	0.022	0.021	0.023
Gujarat	0.175	0.189	0.157	0.163	0.162	0.147	0.165	0.174	0.175
Maharashtra	0.217	0.225	0.213	0.204	0.208	0.195	0.206	0.208	0.200
Andhra Pradesh	0.767	0.782	0.788	0.801	0.820	0.790	0.818	0.841	0.836
Karnataka	0.699	0.705	0.681	0.669	0.699	0.714	0.747	0.770	0.764
Kerala	0.251	0.256	0.240	0.244	0.256	0.267	0.281	0.284	0.275
Tamil Nadu	0.070	0.088	0.078	0.096	0.092	0.090	0.107	0.123	0.136

Source: Author's calculation from secondary data

Continuation of Table-2

States	2001	2002	2003	2004	2005	2006	2007	2007	2008
Haryana	0.223	0.333	0.306	0.253	0.263	0.239	0.287	0.220	10
Himachal Pradesh	0.010	0.010	0.008	0.010	0.012	0.010	0.073	0.016	21
Jammu & Kashmir	0.035	0.039	0.033	0.037	0.034	0.034	0.093	0.043	18
Punjab	0.087	0.092	0.098	0.106	0.109	0.110	0.183	0.086	17
Rajasthan	0.539	0.528	0.530	0.528	0.516	0.493	0.553	0.510	5
Assam	0.151	0.149	0.157	0.159	0.156	0.153	0.219	0.155	13
Tripura	0.016	0.024	0.022	0.026	0.022	0.023	0.086	0.019	20
Bihar	0.683	0.670	0.636	0.623	0.590	0.616	0.701	0.637	4
Jharkhand	0.105	0.106	0.098	0.095	0.089	0.082	0.141	0.112	16
Orissa	0.422	0.414	0.401	0.388	0.360	0.337	0.375	0.405	8
West Bengal	0.402	0.402	0.403	0.399	0.388	0.378	0.424	0.423	7
Chhattisgarh	0.135	0.137	0.131	0.136	0.139	0.139	0.197	0.137	14
Madhya Pradesh	0.516	0.505	0.477	0.459	0.458	0.452	0.491	0.493	6
Uttar Pradesh	1.655	1.642	1.639	1.649	1.643	1.653	1.680	1.645	1
Uttarakhand	0.023	0.028	0.021	0.024	0.028	0.029	0.097	0.027	19
Gujarat	0.175	0.161	0.154	0.165	0.176	0.184	0.250	0.173	12
Maharashtra	0.200	0.207	0.199	0.219	0.226	0.225	0.288	0.215	11
Andhra Pradesh	0.836	0.844	0.880	0.889	0.923	0.911	0.573	0.819	2
Karnataka	0.764	0.788	0.778	0.754	0.759	0.791	0.874	0.747	3
Kerala	0.275	0.289	0.281	0.260	0.293	0.290	0.348	0.275	9
Tamil Nadu	0.136	0.145	0.151	0.165	0.173	0.161	0.231	0.128	15

Source: Author's calculation from secondary data

For the purpose of analytical convenience, values greater than 0.6 are considered as indicative of higher financial inclusion, values within the range (0.3 - 0.6) indicate medium financial inclusion while values less than 0.3 imply lower financial inclusion index. In the year 2001, four states, namely Bihar, Uttar Pradesh, Andhra Pradesh and Karnataka have found place in the category of 'higher level of inclusion' while other four states, such as Rajasthan, Orissa, West Bengal and Madhya Pradesh have been placed in the 'medium level of inclusion' class. Haryana, Himachal Pradesh, Jammu and Kashmir, Punjab, Assam, Tripura, Jharkhand, Chhattisgarh, Uttarakhand, Gujarat, Maharashtra, Kerala, Tamil Nadu have found place in the category of 'lower level of inclusion'.

The study also reveals that during the financial year 2015, Bihar, Uttar Pradesh and Karnataka have been placed in the category of 'higher level of inclusion' while six states, namely Rajasthan, Orissa, West Bengal, Madhya Pradesh, Andhra Pradesh and Kerala have found place in the category of 'medium level of inclusion'. The remaining eleven states (Haryana, Himachal Pradesh, Jammu and Kashmir, Punjab, Assam, Tripura, Jharkhand, Chhattisgarh, Uttarakhand, Gujarat, Maharashtra and Tamil Nadu) have been placed in the category of 'lower level inclusion'. If the performance achieved in the year 2015 is compared with that reached in the initial year of the study period, it is observed that only Kerala has been able to shift itself from the lower level of inclusion cell to the medium level class whereas Andhra Pradesh has failed to retain its status i.e. 'higher level of inclusion' class and has been placed in the medium level class.

On this basis of average value of index it is observed from Table 1 that out of 21 states, 13 states (Haryana, Himachal Pradesh, Jammu and Kashmir, Punjab, Assam, Tripura, Jharkhand, Chhattisgarh, Uttarakhand, Gujarat, Maharashtra, Kerala and Tamil Nadu) have experienced lower level of financial inclusion during the study period. Again four states (Rajasthan, Orissa, West Bengal and Madhya Pradesh) have enjoyed only medium level of inclusion. The states like Bihar, Uttar Pradesh, Andhra Pradesh and Karnataka have enjoyed higher level of inclusion. This finding is plausibly due to a miserable level of development of extension of banking services in such states. *On the whole, looking at the year-wise worst performing states, it can be said that special attention need to be given to the states like* Himachal Pradesh, Jammu and Kashmir, Punjab, Tripura and Uttarakhand. *One significant outcome of the study is that out of 21 states, 18 states have registered rising trend in the value of financial inclusion over time.* It is observed that in the states like Orrisa, west Bengal and Andhra Pradesh the value of financial inclusion index have decreased in the year 2015 as compared to that in 2001.

The analysis of average profitability indices also discloses that Uttar Pradesh has captured the top most position in respect of financial inclusion whereas Andhra Pradesh and Karnataka have secured the second and third positions respectively. The last three positions have been captured by Uttarakhand, Tripura and Himachal Pradesh respectively. Another important outcome of the study is that Uttar Pradesh has secured the highest value of financial inclusion in all the years under study.

CONCLUSION

Financial inclusion is an important element in the way to economic development, poverty reduction and eliminating social exclusion. It is a multidimensional concept that encompasses a number of indicators covering various aspects of peoples' involvement with banking or institutional services. The intensity of financial inclusion is governed both from the supply and demand sides. While on the supply side, the number of branches of banks or ATM facilities indicates efforts of financial authorities to reach people by offering their diverse services, on the demand side the loan availed/ deposits made by people reflect the intensity of desire to use such services.

This study focuses on the aspect of financial inclusion across the selected major states in India. The study reveals wide variations in the level of financial inclusion. In Uttar Pradesh, the value of financial inclusion has exceeded one. Another notable outcome of the study is that in majority of the states, the value of inclusion index has increased over the period under study. However, special attention should be given to the states like Himachal Pradesh, Jammu and Kashmir, Punjab, Tripura and Uttarakhand in order to enhance their status.

REFERENCES:

- Ahmed, J. U. (2015). Performance evaluation of regional rural banks: evidence from Indian rural banks, Global Business Review, 16(5S), 125S–139S.
- *Morduch, J., & Rutherford, S. (2003). Microfinance: analytical issues for India, in PriyaBasu, (eds.), India's Financial Sector: Issues, Challenges and Policy Options. Oxford University Press.*
- Pathak, S. &Raees, S. (2015). Financial inclusion through regional rural banks (RRBs) - dream or reality, Finance Management, 208-213.
- *Rangarajan Committee. (2008). Report of the committee on financial inclusion, Government of India.*
- *Rao, B.P. &Rao, R. B. (2016).Regional rural banks and financial inclusion, Vidyaniketan Journal of Management and Research, 4 (1), 46-63.*
- Reddy, D.M., & Prasad, K.V.N. (2011). Evaluating performance of regional rural banks: an application of camelmodel. Research World, Journal of Arts, Science and Commerce, 2(4), 61-67.
- *Sarma, M. (2008). Index of financial inclusion. Indian Council for Research on International Economic Relations, Working Paper No. 215.*
- *Solo, T. M. (2008). Financial exclusion in Latin America -or the social costs of not banking the urban poor. Environment and Urbanization, 20, 47-66.*

8

The Performance Evaluation of Regional Rural Banks in India: A Comparative Study

Swapan Kumar Biswas

INTRODUCTION

India has a long past history regarding the economic thinking and efforts, starting from the Vedic era continuing to this modern age. At present in every sphere of the economic activities in our country role of banking institution is considered to be indispensible. After nationalization of the commercial banks though their activities have been expanded in many respects but they could not reach to all the corners of our society, specially to the remote areas where a large number of people of the country live mainly based on agriculture and allied activities, who are in real sense economically and socially downtrodden. Ultimately, as a substitute of the commercial banks, the Regional Rural Banks were conceived as the low cost institutions having a rural ethos, local feel and pro-poor focus.

GENESIS OF REGIONAL RURAL BANKS

The first recommendation for establishment of Regional Rural Banks(RRB) was made by Banking Commission in 1972. Thereafter on the basis of recommendation of the Narsimham Working Group, set up by the central Govt., ordinance for RRBs was promulgated on 27th September, 1975 and the RRB Act was passed in 1976.

The RRB concept was based upon the policy that they would lend only to the weaker sections of the society, charging lower interest rates, opening branches in rural and remote areas and keep a low cost profile. RRBs are owned by three entities : Central Govt. 50% State Govt. 15% and sponsor bank 35%.

OBJECTIVES

The major objectives of RRBs may be stated follows:

a) To save the rural poor from the private money lenders.
b) To identify the financial need in the rural areas.
c) To provide cheap and liberal credit facilities mainly to the agro-based people in rural areas.
d) To encourage small entrepreneurship in rural belt.
e) To cultivate the banking habits among the rural people.
f) To enhance banking and financing facilities up to the doorsteps of rural people living in backward and unbanked areas.
g) To increase employment opportunities by encouraging trade and commerce in rural and semi-urban areas
h) To act as a catalyst element and thereby accelerate the economic growth in the particular region.

JOURNEY OF THE RRBs FOR FIRST TWO-DECADES

The journey was sorrowful.

At the initial stage the banks expanded very fast and by the end of 1985 RRBs had opened 12606 branches. But within the first ten years period after establishment of the first RRB (Prathama Gramin Bank, U.P.) most of the branches were making losses, their credit deposit ratio was continuously declined and the original assumptions as the low cost nature of these institutions were belied. The questions started being raised about the viability of the banks.

In 1989, the Khusru Committee (The Agricultural Credit Review Committee) noted the weakness of the RRBs, particularly their inability to sustain due to mounting losses and opined for merger with the sponsor banks.

In 1990 the Narsimham Committee also recommended for merger of the RRBs with their sponsor banks. By 1993, out of 196 RRBs 172 were recorded unprofitable. Some measures were taken up by the Reserve Bank of India for strengthening the financial structure of the RRBs.

- It allowed RRBs to relocate their branches if they were incurring losses for more than three years at one location.
- The RRBs were also allowed to finance non-target group to the extent not exceeding 4o percent of their lending, which subsequently enhanced to 60 percent in 1994.
- As a result RRBs diversified their activities--made advances to the non - priority sector including jewel, deposit linked loans, consumer loans and home loans.

PROCESS OF RECAPITALIZATION AND AMALGAMATION

In the wake of introduction of financial sector reforms in 1991-92, the commercial viability of RRBs emerged as the most crucial factor in deciding about their desired role due to their limited business flexibility with hardly any scope of expansion, smaller size of loans with higher exposure to risk-prone advances and professional efficiency in financial deployment . To strengthen RRBs and improve their performance many initiatives have taken by the Govt. of India and RBI.

- Recapitalization of RRBs was initiated in 1994-95 and continued till 1999-2000. Financial support extended to 187 RRBs with aggregate amount Rs. 2188.44 crore by shareholders.
- RRBs were allowed to undertake Government business including foreign exchange business with the permission of the Govt. and RBI.
- RRBs have been permitted to merge/close down their unviable branches.

  In 2001, a committee under the chairmanship of Dr. V.S. Vyas was constituted by the RBI(The expert committee on Rural Credit) which examined relevance of RRBs in the rural credit system and recommended(2004) for consolidation and amalgamation of RRBs for making them viable.
- The first phase of amalgamation was initiated sponsor Bank wise within a state in 2005 and the second phase was across the sponsor banks within a state in 2012.
- The process was initiated with a view to provide better customer services by having better infrastructure, computerization, experienced work force, common publicity, marketing efforts, etc.
- As a result of amalgamation, the number of RRBs has been reduced from 196 (March, 1990) to 64 (March, 2013) and thereafter to 56 (March, 2015).

Capital to Risk weighted Assets Ratio(CRAR) is a very important yard-stick for measuring the financial structure of a bank. But in the early 2000s there was no importance to measure and maintain CRAR for RRBs.

For the first time in 2005, an internal working group recommended for maintaining 5% CRAR by all RRBs. Subsequently in 2009, the Union Finance Ministry constituted a committee under the chairmanship of K.C. Chakraborty, Deputy Governor, RBI to analyse the financial position of RRBS and give suggestions for their improvement.

- The committee recommended (in 2010) that out of 82 RRBs 40 should be recapitalized for strengthening their CRAR to the level of 9% by 31 March, 2012. The remaining 42 RRBs are in a position to achieve the desired level of CRAR at their own.
- The recommendation was accepted and the Govt. of India alongwith other shareholders divided to infuse funds to the extent of Rs. 2200 crore for strengthening the RRBs.
- As on 31 March, 2014 an amount of Rs. 2173.43 crore have been released to 38 RRBs in 20 states including Rs. 96.92 crore released as an additional recapitalization fund to Central Madhya Pradesh Gramin Bank.
- U.P. State Govt did not release any amount in respect of remaining 2 RRBs, identified by the committee, in that state.

PERFORMANCES OF RRBs-EVALUATION AND DISCUSSION:

This study is mainly an attempt to compare and evaluate the performances of the RRBs in India for pre-amalgamation(2005) and post-amalgamation periods in terms of some specific parameters, such as, Growth of RRBs, Fund component, Deposit mobilization, Loans and Advances made, Recovery rate, maintenance of CRAR and Profitability and Viability of RRBs.

Growth of Regional Rural Bank in India:

After enactment of the Act, 1976, the RRBs were set up as state-sponsored, regionally based and rural oriented financial institutions. The growth of RRBs in terms of number, branches opened, area covered, is shown in Table-1.

In the year 2003-04, the number of RRBs was 196 with 14,446 branches covering their activities in 518 districts in the country. But from the year 2004-05, as the effect of merger and amalgamation (2005) , the number of RRBs became decreasing and it reduced to 56 in 2014-15.

As regards number of branches opened and number of districts covered there was a slow progress in the years from 2003-04 to 2005-06 but there was a significant growth for the period from 2012-13 to 2015-16.

In 2015-16, the number of RRBs was 56 with 20904 branches covering 644 districts in the Country. Thus, it can be said that the process of amalgamation has a direct effect in the growth of the RRBs in post-amalgamation period.

Table-1: Growth of Regional Rural Bank in India by number, coverage & manpower

Year	Number of RRBs	Number of Branches	No. of District Covered	No. of staff employed
2003-04	196	14446	518	69249
2004-05	133	14484	523	68912
2005-06	94	14494	525	68629
2012-13	64	17861	635	76246
2013-14	57	19082	642	80075
2014-15	56	20024	644	NA
2015-16	56	20904	644	NA

Sources: Dept. of Financial services, Ministry of Finance, Govt. of India & NABARD Annual Reports

Capital composition of the RRBs

One of the main objectives of setting up of RRBs was to provide cheap and liberal credit facilities in the rural areas. But for extending the credit facilities and maintaining the progress of growth sound financial position of the bank is essential. RRBs have two types of fund, i.e. owned fund and borrowed fund. The owned fund of the RRBs comprising Share Capital, Share Capital Deposits received from the Shareholders and Reserve and Surplus created out of the net profit earned by the Bank. Whereas, in the borrowed fund, borrowing from NABARD constitutes the major share. The other sources of borrowings are Sponsor Bank, SIDBI, National Housing Bank etc.

Table -2 exhibits that there was a growth of owned fund by 22.23 % between 2003-04 and 2005-06 whereas, that growth was 41 % between 2012-13 and 2015-16. This reveals the increasing trend in the growth rate of owned fund in post amalgamation period.

On the other hand the growth of borrowed fund was by 58.93 % between 2003-04 and 2005-06 whereas, that growth was 26.36 % between

2012-13 and 2015-16. This reveals the decreasing trend in the growth rate of borrowed fund in post amalgamation period.

Besides the above, in the total capital component of the RRBs the borrowed fund has possessed tha major share with its gradual increase which can be observed from that table. The percentage of owned fund and borrowed fund which were 54.20% and 45.80% respectively in 2003-04, came to 36.30% and 63.70% respectively in 2015-16. This kind of too much dependence on borrowed fund is not healthy for the prudent financial structure of a banking institution.

Table-2: Component of total fund of RRBs. (Rs. in crore)

Year	Total Fund	Owned Fund	% of Total Fund	Borrowed Fund	% of Total Fund
2003-04	10033	5438	54.20	4595	45.80
2004-05	11705	6181	52.80	5524	47.20
2005-06	13950	6647	47.65	7303	52.35
2012-13	57518	19445	33.80	38073	66.20
2013-14	72402	22172	30.62	50230	69.38
2014-15	84506	25084	29.68	59422	70.32
2015-16	75530	27420	36.30	48110	63.70

Sources: Dept. of Financial services, Ministry of Finance, Govt. of India & NABARD Annual Reports.

Credit Deposit Ratio (C-D Ratio)

RRBs were established with the objectives to cultivate the banking habits among the rural people and to enhance banking and financing facilities up to their door-steps. The Credit Deposit Ratio of the RRB indicates the creation of credit out of the deposits mobilized by the banks in the rural belt of their operation.

Table-3 exhibits that there was a constant increasing trend in C-D Ration during the pre-amalgamation period from 2003-04 to 2005-06 as well as post-amalgamation period from 2012-13 to 2015-16.

In 2003-04 the CD Ratio of RRBs was 46.34% which has been increased to 65.79% in 2015-16. In 2013-14 this rate was the highest, i.e. 66.55% among the data given in the table for different years.

This result implies that the deposits mobilized by the RRBs have been used properly by the banks for extending credit facilities in the rural areas, though there is still a scope of further improvement in this ratio.

Table-3: Deposits, Loans and Advances, C.D. Ratio & Loan Recovery of RRBs. (Rs in crore)

Year	Deposits	Loans & Advances O/S	C.D. Ratio	Recovery % (as on 30 June of previous year)
2003-04	56350	26114	46.34	NA
2004-05	62143	32870	52.89	NA
2005-06	71329	39713	55.67	NA
2012-13	211488	139652	66.03	81.17
2013-14	239494	159406	66.55	81.90
2014-15	273018	180955	66.27	79.49
2015-16	315048	207279	65.79	82.51

Sources: Dept. of Financial services, Ministry of Finance, Govt. of India & NABARD Annual Reports

Recovery of outstanding loans

The RRB concept was based upon the policy that they would lend to the weaker sections of the rural society charging lower interest rates. But the extension of loan facilities, maintenance of financial health and sustenance of the existence of RRBs, recovery of loan plays a very important part in their operation.

Table-3 exhibits that the recovery performance of RRBs has a steady improvement over the post-amalgamation period. The recovery rate which was 81.17% as on 30 June, 2012 has been increased to 82.51% as on 30 June, 2015. State wise recovery performance of RRBs as on 30 June, 2014 has been shown in Table-4. Twenty one out of 56 RRBs had a recovery level above the all India average with 9 RRBs above 90% . Thirty five RRBs had recovery level less than 80% with two RRBs having a level of less that 60%. This position has changed slightly in the year 2015-16.

However, in absolute terms the overdues have increased from Rs. 26114 crore in 2003-04 to Rs. 139652 croreas on 30 June, 2012 and to Rs. 2,07279 crore as on 30 June, 2015

So, despite the improvement of recovery performance of RRBs in terms of percentage, the total amount of overdues has been mounted during the post-amalgamation period. Measures should be adopted for recovery of the outstanding loans, because effective recovery of loans is the backbone of any financial institution.

Table-4: Frequency Distribution of states according to level of recovery of outstanding loans of RRBs as on 30 June, 2014

Sl. No.	Recovery Range(%)	States
1	>90	Bihar (2), Kerala (1), Puduchery (1), Punjab (3), Tamil Nadu (2), [Total = 9]
2	80 to 90	Gujarat (2), Haryana (1), Himachal Pradesh (1), Karnataka (1), M.P. (1), Maharashtra (1), Rajasthan (1), U.P. (2), Uttarakhand (1), West Bengal (1) [Total = 12]
3	60 to <80	Andhra Pradesh (4), Arunachal Pradesh (1), Assam (2), Bihar (1), Chhattishgarh (1), Gujarat (1), J&K (2), Jharkhand (1), Karnataka (2), Maharashtra (1), M.P. (2), Mnipur (1), Meghalaya (1), Mizoram (1), Odisha (2), Rajasthan (1), Telangana (1), Tripura (1), U.P. (5), West Bengal (2) [Total = 33]
4	<60	Jharkhand (1), Nagaland (1) [Total = 2]

- The number of RRBs as on 30 June, 2014 was 56
- Figures in the parenthesis indicate the number of RRBs

Financing of small and marginal farmers

The main objective of setting up of the RRBs was to provide credit and other facilities particularly to the small and marginal farmers, agricultural labourers, etc. , who are primarily agro-based people of the rural areas. But how far this objective has been fulfilled by this time, that can be understood from the Table-5.

From the comparative table (Table-5) we shall be able to find out that among the three agencies, commercial banks, cooperative banks and RRBs, the Regional Rural Banks had the highest share of disbursement of loans to the small and marginal farmers both in terms of number of account holders and amount disbursed in relation to their total disbursement.

In 2013-14, for RRBs 67.11% of total accounts were pertaining to small and marginal farmers and 62.14% of total loan amount disbursed were also given to small and marginal farmers. For commercial banks and co-operative banks these ratios were at a lower level.

But as regards total amount of loan disbursed to the small and marginal farmers and accounts opened in their names by all the three agencies the performance of RRBs secured the third position among the three agencies.

So, RRBs have to take more initiative for extending credit facilities in the rural areas for the benefit of the agro-based people of that belt.

Table-5: Loan disbursed to Small/Marginal farmers during the year 2013-14 by three agencies (No. in Lac & Amount in Crore)

Sl. No	Agency	No. of A/Cs	Disbursed Amount Total	A/Cs pertaining to SF/MF	% share to total Number of A/Cs	Credit disbursed to SF/MF	% share to total credit disbursed
1	Comm. Banks	379.04	509004.96	234.52	61.87	201296.26	39.55
2	Coop. Banks	321.37	119963.79	206.05	64.12	69352.24	57.81
3	RRBs	99.27	82652.72	66.62	67.11	51358.81	62.14
Total		799.68	711621.47	507.19	63.42	322007.31	42.25

Sources: Dept. of Financial services, Ministry of Finance, Govt. of India

Capital to Risk weighted Assets Ratio (CRAR)

The main cause for recapitalization of RRBs after amalgamation was their financial weakness due to having high non-performing assets as well as a very low capital to risk weighted assets ratio (CRAR). For maintaining the financial stability, Chakraborty Committee recommended to achieve 9% CRAR by 31 March, 2012. Thereafter RBI had also advised to RRBs to maintain a minimum level of CRAR of 9% with effect from 31 March, 2014.

Table-6 shows that in 2012-13 out of 64 RRBs 61 (i.e. 95.31%) attained the required level of 9% CRAR which became comparatively low in 2014-15 where out of 56 RRBs 52(i.e. 92.85%) attained the required level. (Maximum 20.29% CRAR for Chhatisgarh Gramin Bank and minimum 4.82% CRAR for Nagaland Gramin Bank)

For comparing with the institutions operating in the same field with similar objectives, it can be seen from the Annual Report of NABARD as on 31 March 2015, that 2 out of 33 StCBs and 66 out of 371 DCCBs couldn't attain the statutory requirement of 7 % CRAR as notified by RBI.

While RRBs seem to maintain a better CRAR than StCBs and DCCBs, a few RRBs (4 in number) have fallen into lower CRAR bands as on 31 March, 2015.So, there is a need for raising capital fund of the RRBs by earning profit or otherwise, particularly whose performance is below the required level.

Table-6: Status of capital to Risk weighted Asset Ratio (CRAR) in RRBs. Position as on 31 March (No. of RRBs)

Sl. No.	Range of CRAR	2012-13 (23.03% to (-) 8.97%)	2013-14 (19.88% to 3.86%)	2014-15 (20.29% to 4.82%)
1	9% & above	61	56	52
2	7% to <9%	1	0	2
3	5% to <7%	1	0	1
4.	1% to <5%	0	1	1
5	<1%	1	0	0
Total		64	57	56

Sources: NABARD Annual Reports 2014-15 & 2015-16

Table-7: Status of CRAR in StCBs as on 31 March

Sl. No.	Range of CRAR	2012-13	2013-14	2014-15
1	9% & above	17	19	18
2	7% to <9%	7	7	10
3	4% to <7%	6	6	0
4	<4%	2	0	1
Total		32	32	29*

Sources: NABARD Annual Reports

*Data available for 29 St CBs only in 2014-15 out of 33 StCBs

StCBs = State Co-operative Banks.

Table-8: Status of CRAR in DCCBs as on 31 March

Sl. No.	Range of CRAR	2012 - 13	2013 - 14	2014 - 15
1	9% and above	208	222	221
2	7% to <9%	70	77	97
3	4% to <7%	47	45	13
4	<4%	45	24	23
Total		370	368	354*

Sources: NABARD Annual Reports

*Data available for 354 and not available for 17 DCCBs in 2014-15

DCCBs = District Central Co-operative Banks

Profitability and Viability of the RRBs:

The objective of serving the weaker sections of the society by the RRBs can be achieved effectively only by the self-sustaining banks. Before amalgamation most of the RRBs were finding themselves unable to sustain because of the mounting losses due to imprudent commercial policy. After consolidation and amalgamation the picture has been changed to a great extent

The table-9 exhibits that during 2015-16 out of 56 RRBs 51 earned profits while 5 RRBs incurred losses. These numbers were 63 as profit earning and 1 as loss incurring out of 64 RRBs in 2012-13. In 213-14 all RRBs were profit earning

The overall net profit of the RRBs as an agency increased from Rs. 2273 crore as on 31 March, 2013 to Rs. 2434 crore as on 31 March, 2016, but this profit was Rs. 2744 crore in 2014-15. So, the overall net profit has been increased in 2015 – 16 in respect to 2012 - 13 but decreased in respect to the previous year 2014-15.

As regards number of sustainable RRBs, i.e. earning profit and carrying no accumulated losses decreased from 53 out of 64 RRBs as on 31 March, 2013 to 48 out of 56 RRBs as on 31 March, 2016, and there was an amount of Rs. 1030 crore of accumulated losses as on 31 March, 2016.

So, measures should be adopted for making all the RRBs sustainably viable by setting off all the accumulated losses through earning profit regularly.

Table-9: Profitability and Viability of the RRBs(Amount of Rs in crore)

Indicator	2012-13	2013-14	2014-15	2015-16
No. of RRBs	64	57	56	56
RRBs earning profit (No.)	63	57	51	51
RRBs incurring losses (No.)	01	00	05	05
Amount of profit for the year	2275	2694	2921	2556
Amount of Loss for the year	02	00	177	122
Amount of Net Profit for the year	2273	2694	2744	2434
Accumulated Losses	1091	949	1072	1030
RRBs with accumulated losses	11	08	08	08

Sources: Dept. of Financial services, Ministry of Finance, Govt. of India & NABARD Annual Reports

SUGGESTIONS AND RECOMMENDATIONS FOR IMPROVEMENT OF RRBs

1. The unique role of RRBs in providing credit facilities to weaker sections of the villagers must be preserved. The RRBs must exist as rural banks of the rural people.
2. The RRBs must strengthen effective credit administration by way of credit appraisal, monitoring the progress of loans and their effective recovery.
3. The RRBs may relax their lending procedure and make them easy for village borrowers.
4. The RRBs may initiate new insurable policies, like deposit linked Animal insurance policy. Crop insurance policy, Life insurance policy for rural depositors.
5. The RRBs should take necessary step to increase non-interest income by way of locker facilities, collection of cheques and bills, acting as agent, and so on.
6. Participation of local people in the equity share capital of RRBs should be allowed and encouraged on the basis of the RRBs Amendment Act, 2015 for raising capital from sources other than the existing shareholders.
7. Local staff may be appointed in the RRBs as far as possible, so that they can interact more with their customers to overcome the problems of the area.
8. There is a need for proper planning with specific objective after considering the potential and peculiar characteristics of people in the area of operation by the RRBs.

9. There is an urgent need for establishment of 'Research Cell' at the level of H.O. of every RRB for effective and continuous planning, research and development of the institution.
10. Programme of business promotion in terms of 'Awareness Programme' should be organized frequently by the RRBs to overcome the social, cultural and spiritual constraints of the area of operation.

CONCLUSION

In this study an attempt has been made to evaluate the performance of Regional Rural Bank in India for pre-amalgamation and post-amalgamation periods in terms of some specific parameters. Such as, growth of RRBs, Fund component, Deposit Mobilization, Loans and Advances made, Recovery Rate, Capital to Risk weighted Assets Ratio and Profitability and Viability of the RRBs.

It has been seen that during post-amalgamation period, number of RRBs has been decreased but number of branches, districts coverage and all the financial activities, as considered in the study have been increased to a great extent. At the same time the amount of outstanding loans and advances and the accumulated losses have also been increased, which require special attention for adopting proper measures of their recovery or setting off. The CRAR is comparatively better for RRBs than StCBs and DCCBs but it is less than the performance of commercial banks. Efforts should be made for increasing CRAR level of the RRBs

The RRBs should take initiative for extending banking facilities not only to the agricultural sector but also to small entrepreneurs, village and cottage industries for increasing their income which is the precondition for becoming sustainably viable of financial institutions. Installation of ATMs in suitable places of the rural areas will help the RRBs for attracting the existing customers more as well as prospective customers also towards the activities of the bank which will definitely yield good result in future.

REFERENCES

1. Sundaram and Varshney, Banking and Financial System, Sultan Chand and Sons, New Delhi, 2005.
2. Thakur, S. ,Two Decades of Indian Banking: The Service Sector Scenario, Chanakya Publication, New Delhi, 1990.
3. Chakrabarti, Manas, Rural Banking in India, New Century Publications, New Delhi, 2011.
4. Ranga Reddy, A., Rural Banking and Overdues Mnagement, Mittal Publication, New Delhi, 2004.

5. Muraleedharan, D., Modern Banking: Theory and Practice, PHI Learning Pvt. Ltd., New Delhi, 2009.
6. Sonara, C. K., Regional Rural Bank in India, Anmol Publications (P) Ltd., New Delhi, 1988.
7. Sabitha Devi, N., Problems and Prospects of Regional Rural Bank in India, International Journal of Managerial Studies and Research, April, 2014, Vol. 2, Issue 3, PP 69 – 72.
8. Syed Ibrahim, Dr. M., Performance Evaluation of Regional Rural Banks in India, Internation Bussiness Reseach, October, 2010, Vol. 3, No. 4, PP 203 – 211.
9. Jagadeesh, P. , Problems of Regional Rural Bank in India, Journal for Advanced Research in Commerce and Management, 2014, Vol. 1, Issue 1, PP 47 – 50.
10. Bose, S. , Regional Rural Banks in India: The Past and the Present Debates, 2005, Macroscan, Retrived from http://www.macroscan.com/fet/jul 05/fet 2007 05 RRB ___ Debate. htm.
11. NABARD Annual Reports, 2014 – 15 and 2015 – 16.
12. Report on RRBs as on 31 March, 2014, Department of Financial Services, Ministry of Finance, Govt. of India.

9

Management of NPA of RRBs in India- A Hard Rock to Drill

Goutam Sinha
Goutam Chatterjee
Uday Chand Das

INTRODUCTION

Non Performing Assets are those assets which remain non operational within the organization. Non operational means no contribution in earning income for the organization. Moreover, its presence indicates subsequent losses to be written off from profit. In other words, it means that if a borrower of a bank is not paying the interest on loan and the principal amount in time, it becomes a non performing asset of the bank.

Before 31st March 2001, the practice was to consider NPA as "past due". An amount was considered as "past due" when it had remained outstanding for 30 days beyond the due date. An asset is considered non-performing when it fails to generate any income for the bank.

Loans & advances given by a bank to the borrowers are assets to the bank. This asset or loan is classified as:

1. Standard assets (for which the borrowers pay their dues regularly and on time)

2. Substandard assets (those, which have remained NPA for a period less than or equal to 12 months)
3. Doubtful assets (doubtful assets are those remaining in the substandard category for a period of 12 months)
4. Loss assets (loss asset is one for which loss has been identified by bank, or by internal or external auditors or by RBI through inspection)\

A loss asset is considered uncollectable and as such it is to be written off.

As per guidelines of RBI, an NPA is defined as a loan and advance where:

1. Interest and / or installment of principal remain overdue for a period of 90 days in respect of a term loan.
2. The account remains 'out of order' in respect of an overdraft or cash credit.
3. The bills remain overdue for a period of more than 90 days in case of a bill purchased and discounted.
4. The installment of principal or interest thereon remains overdue for two crop seasons for short duration crops.
5. The installment of principal or interest thereon remains overdue for one crop season for long duration crops.
6. The amount of liquidity facility remains outstanding for more than 90 days in respect of a securitization transaction undertaken in terms of guidelines of securitization dated, February 1st, 2006.
7. In respect of derivative transactions, the overdue receivables representing positive market to market value of a derivative contract, if they remain unpaid for a period of 90 days from the specified due date for payment.

Non-performing assets adversely affect the profitability of the commercial banks. It also affects the operational efficiency of a banker. NPA has both direct and indirect impacts on the banking sector.

Direct impacts of NPA

1. It may affect the profitability of the unit significantly. In case of branch banking, some units performed well and make a major contribution to the profitability as a whole. But due to NPA, some branches become loss-making units and bearing such losses, the organizational performance as a whole shows a very little positive profit.
2. It affects the credibility of the bank. Due to NPA, bankers fail to meet financial commitments and promises made.

3. It affects the recycling of funds.

Indirect impacts of NPA

1. Reduction in risk taking ability which ultimately affects negatively the competitive power of the banking units.
2. It affects to curb the credit expansion ability of banking units. Due to the cost of poor quality loans and advances, the banking activities are hampered to a great extent.
3. Reduction in lending rate is made difficult.

Now, our paper is related to the management of NPAs of Regional Rural Banks in India.

About the Regional Rural Banks of India

As per Ordinance passed in September, 1975 and the RRB Act 1976, the Regional Rural Bank came into existence. It has started its journey on 2nd October, 1975 to include rural areas into the main economic stream. The main objective of RRBs is to provide sufficient banking credit facilities to the agriculture and other rural sectors.

RRBs are local level banking organizations operating in different states of India. At present, RRBs do not confine their area of activities only to the rural people but to the semi-urban and urban areas. As per present scenario, 56 RRBs are functioning in different states in India by providing banking facilities to rural, semi-urban and urban areas along with Govt. operation, like disbursement of wages of MGNREGA workers, disbursement of pensions etc. and para- banking facilities, like Locker facilities, debit & credit cards etc.

OBJECTIVES OF THE STUDY

- The first and foremost objective of the study is to show the trend of NPA during the period under study and to compare with the Nationalized Banks in India.
- To show the existence of NPA and its share in the gross outstanding loan of RRBs during the period under study.
- To get the effect of NPA on Owner's equity.
- To show its effect on operational activities of the unit under study.

Methodology

Methodology to be used in a study depends on purposes to be served. Keeping in mind the said principle, some simple mathematical techniques like, average, percentage etc. and the technique of ratio analysis have been used to analyse the data during the study period.

Study Plan

In order to have detailed picture, a comparatively long period of ten years i.e, from 2004-2005 to 2013-2014 is taken as study period. We think that the period is sufficient enough for the purpose of analysis of relevant data.

Data Source

The data used in this study have been collected from website of regional rural banks of India and also from the different well-known journals, annual reports of the banks published time to time.

Limitations of the study

The main limitation of the study is the use of secondary data. The data used in this study has been collected from secondary sources. The difficulties for the use of secondary data are well-known to us. The second limitation is the techniques used for the analysis of data.

Table-1: Size of NPA of RRBs & Nationalized Banks in India during the period under study

Year	RRBs in India		Nationalized Banks in India	
	NPA(crore)	% of growth	NPA(crore)	% of growth
2004-2005	2795	-	46817	-
2005-2006	2947	5.43	41378	-11.62
2006-2007	3178	7.84	38305	-7.43
2007-2008	3566	12.21	39600	3.38
2008-2009	2804	-21.37	44032	11.19
2009-2010	3085	10.02	57293	30.12
2010-2011	3712	20.32	71080	24.06
2011-2012	5859	57.84	112489	58.26
2012-2013	8330	29.66	155890	38.58
2013-2014	9657	15.92	204215	31.15

From the above table, it is revealed that the size of NPA of RRBs is steadily increasing throughout the period under study except in the year 2008-2009. But while considering the percentage of growth, it is steadily increasing up to2011-2012 except in the year 2008-2009 and thereafter decreasing. But, in case of Nationalized Banks, the size of NPA is increasing since 2007-2008. At the initial stage of the study period, the rate of growth was registered as negative and thereafter increasing positively. During the last five years of the study period, in both the cases show the same scenario (volume is increasing but the rate of growth is declining).

Table-2: This table shows the size of NPA & O/S Gross loan during the study period (in Crore rupees)

Year	NPA (Crore)	Gross Loan (O/S)	% of NPA on Gross Loan (O/S)
2004-2005	2795	37817	7.39
2005-2006	2947	42361	6.96
2006-2007	3178	48492	6.55
2007-2008	3566	58984	6.04
2008-2009	2804	67858	4.15
2009-2010	3085	82819	3.72
2010-2011	3712	98917	3.75
2011-2012	5859	116385	5.03
2012-2013	8330	139652	5.96
2013-2014	9657	159302	6.06

From the above table it is seen that the amount of gross outstanding loan is increasing with the passage of time along with the increase in NPA during the study period. But the percentage of NPA on Gross outstanding loan is decreasing continuously up to 2010-11 and thereafter increasing steadily for the rest of the study period.

Table-3: Size of GNPA & Net Worth of the RRBs in India during the study period

Year	GNPA(crore)	Net Worth	%
2004-2005	2795	3597	78.09
2005-2006	2947	4212	69.97
2006-2007	3178	4526	70.22
2007-2008	3566	6107	58.39
2008-2009	2804	8570	32.72
2009-2010	3085	10472	29.45
2010-2011	3712	12307	30.16
2011-2012	5859	15129	38.72
2012-2013	8330	18355	45.38
2013-2014	9657	21200	45.55

From the above table, it is found that the percentage of GNPA in Net Worth (Owners fund) is showing declining trend up to 2009-10 and thereafter it is increasing. Increase in percentage in this regard indicates the indirect threat to the owner's fund.

CONCLUSION

It is concluded that the size of NPA of RRBs is gradually increasing with the periods to come and the rate of growth is also increasing in most of the years of the study period. The same picture is also found in case of Nationalized Banks of India. In other words, it is said that the RRBs in India maintains the Uniformity with the Nationalized Banks of India.

The percentage of NPA of RRBs in India in Net Worth has also registered an increasing trend throughout the period under study. It implies indirectly a threat to the owner's equity. In spite of taking different improved measures, it is not controlled at the desired level.

The percentage of NPA of RRBs in India on gross outstanding loan is found as steadily increasing during the last part of the study period. This matter indicates the inefficiency of the bankers in realizing the loan in time. This may be the cause for swelling up of the NPA.

REMEDIAL MEASURES

The management of NPA in banks is very difficult. Sweeping the problems under the carpet is not a solution. To make this journey successful, the banks must have to strengthen their credit appraisal standards and to put greater focus on the quantum of equity brought in by the promoters. The appraisal and approval process for restructuring proposals needs to be improved while ensuring that the benefits of restructuring are also extended to the small borrowers. Some suggested measures in this regard are –

1. Prudential Norms and regulations suggested by RBI and credit quality are highly correlated. Soft and flip-flox approach to regulation may have contribution to the creation of NPA and stressed assets. The bankers must have to be cautious in this regard.
2. Process of recognizing NPA must be very quick and aggressive which helps to develop better management of NPA.
3. High space of credit growth in certain segments has resulted in lower credit quality in those segments. The bank has to avoid such strategy as much as practicable.
4. Timely action based on information needs to be taken everywhere to recovery the loans and advances.
5. Standard and quality of credit management as well as recovery management give much strengthen to the bankers to reduce the quantum of NPA which is a parameter for future growth and development.

REFERENCES

1. N.R. Mohan Prakash, Banking, Risk And Insurance Management, Vikash Publising House Pvt Ltd., New Delhi, 2016
2. A. Sudarshana Reddy and Prof. A. Padmavathi (2013), Growth and Performance of Regional Rural Banks in India, international Journal of Scientific Research, volume 2, November 2013, pp. 119-120.
3. NABARD official websites.
4. Annual Reports of RRBs.

10

Financial Sector Reforms & the Functioning of Regional Rural Banks in India

Partha Pratim Roy

INTRODUCTION

In an agrarian economy like India the Regional Rural Banks play a vital role. Rapid growth in agriculture is essential both for self-reliance and earning valuable foreign exchange. Indian farmers are second to none in production and productivity despite the fact that millions are marginal and small farmers. The Working Group on rural banks (1975) recommended the establishment of Regional Rural Banks to supplement the efforts of the commercial banks. The main objective of the Regional Rural Banks is to provide credit and other facilities particularly to the small and marginal farmers, agricultural laborers, artisans and small entrepreneurs so as to develop agriculture, trade, commerce industry and other productive activities in the rural areas. These rural banks were an endeavor in this direction to create a platform for meeting all informational needs relating to Agriculture, Animal Husbandry and Fisheries sectors production, sale/storage of an Indian farmer.

The development process of RRBs started on 2 October 1975 with the forming of the first RRB, the Prathama Bank with authorised capital of Rs. 5 crore at its starting. Also on 2 October 1976 five regional rural banks were set up with a total authorised capital Rs. 100 crore ($10 Million) only.

From 2nd October 1975 the number of RRB's has increased from 5 to 196 in 2008-09. A survey conducted by RBI in 1981 stated that "the basic aim of setting up RRB's viz. developing the rural economy by providing credit for the development of agriculture, trade, commerce industry and other productive activities in rural areas was being fulfilled." Before the financial sector reforms in India, according to the RBI, the RRB's have fared well in achieving the weaker the objective of providing access to sections of the society to institutional credit but the recovery position on the whole is not satisfactory. In the pre-reform period RRB's were expected to revolutionize rural banking by bringing in all the advantages of commercial banks to the door steps of the small and marginal farmer. But it did not happen. After 1991 different committees were set up to visualize the functioning of the role of RRB's and its performance. Some problems of RRB's are organizational, problems related to recovery, management problems and problems of mounting losses leading to non-viability. Narasimham Committee (1991) recommended different opinions. Thereafter different policies were taken and different actions were taken by the government of India. An attempt has been made in this paper to discuss the present condition of functioning of RRB's in India.

Rural people of India have their own traditional convention and ethos. It is very hard to make them convince in introduction of every social and economical aspects from time to time. As far as financial sector is concerned it is the toughest job to make them educate in bringing up under the umbrella of a sound banking system. So a separate group of banks were needed to cater to the needs of the rural people. Regional rural banks serve basically those targeted group.

Structure of Regional Rural Banks

The Regional Rural Bank were owned by the Central Government, the State Government and the Sponsor Bank(There were five commercial banks, Punjab National Bank, State Bank of India, Syndicate Bank, United Bank of India and United Commercial Bank, which sponsored the regional rural banks) who held shares in the ratios as follows Central Government-50%, State Government- 15% and Sponsor Banks- 35%.. Earlier, Reserve Bank of India had laid down ceilings on the rate of interest to be charged by these RRBs.

At first in 1975 five R.R.B's were set up in the following places:

Moradabad & Gorakhpur in U.P., Jaipur in RAJASTHAN, Viwani in HARIYANA and Malda in WEST BENGAL.

The RRBs mobilize financial resources from rural/semi-urban areas and grant loans and advances mostly to small and marginal farmers, agricultural labourers and rural artisans. The area of operation of RRBs is limited to the area as notified by Govt. of India covering one or more districts in the State. This paper focuses the following:-

a) The difference between the commercial banks and regional rural banks.
b) Financial sector reforms and RRB's
c) The difference between the pre and post reform era regarding the objective of the RRB's
d) A brief snapshot of the recommendations of different committees.

Difference between commercial banks & Regional Rural Banks

The main reason behind the existence of RRB is the development of rural and backward areas, and also providing banking facility to rural population whereas the commercial banks is to make profits out of their operations. The scope of RRB is limited to agriculture finance, small sector loans, handicrafts and other small sector loans, but the scope of commercial banks being wide it not only provides loan for agricultural purposes but also for financing housing loan, car loan credit to big companies etc. RRB's are at present in rural and semi urban areas only whereas commercial banks do operations in all over the country that is rural, semi urban and urban. While the focus of RRB is more on accepting deposits and granting of loans to the people whereas the focus of commercial banks apart from lending and borrowing is on many other services like stock broking merchant banking etc. Stakeholders of RRB's are: Government of India, State government and commercial banks whereas stakeholders of commercial banks are public, central government etc.

So we can say the following:-

i) The area of operation of RRB's is limited to a specific region within a specified block of a rural area.
ii) RRB's provide direct loans and advances to small & marginal farmers, rural artisans, & agricultural labors to increase the production of the rural economy.
iii) The lending rates of RRB's is not higher than the prevailing lending rates of co-operatives.
iv) The sponsoring banks & RBI provide subsidies and concessions to RRB have to enable the function of RRB.

Financial Sector Reforms

Financial sector is the backbone of any country and it plays a crucial role in the mobilization and allocation of resources. Traditionally commercial banks were the main source of finance. Later after the establishment of the Regional Rural Banks in the mid 80's RRB's have also certain roles in the Indian economy. The basic objective of any financial reform process is to formulate the policy for improving the financial health and to strengthen the institutions. In India the main objectives of the financial sector reform process initiated in the early 1990s were the following:-

1. To get rid of the excessive regulation and financial repression with a view to create an atmosphere conducive to the emergence of an efficient, productive and profitable financial sector.
2. To enable the growth of financial markets that would enhance new prices, new interest rates by the market dynamics that in turn will help in efficient allocation of resources.
3. To provide operational and functional autonomy to institutions to facilitate the growth of a robust financial system.
4. To Open up the external sector in a calibrated fashion so that the domestic sector could withstand the challenges from international financial system.
5. To prepare the financial entities to deal with the impulses arising from the developments in the global economy by promoting measures of financial stability, which emerged as an important objective of monetary policy along with price stability and economic growth.

So basically the reform process initiated aimed at the following:-

i) Interest rate liberalization

ii) Reduction in reserve requirements

iii) Entry regulation

iv) Credit Policies

FEATURES OF RRBs DURING REFORM PERIOD

The Govt. of India in consultation with RBI and NABARD started the reform process with a comprehensive package for RRBs when the reforms started in the Banking sector. It included cleansing their balance sheets and recapitalising them. Extant lending restrictions were removed and space and variety available for investment of their surplus funds was expanded.

Simultaneously, with funding support of the Swiss Development Corporation (SDC) a number of human resource development initiatives were taken up by NABARD with training and exposure visits, Organisational Development Initiatives, technology support, computerization and use of IT, system development, etc. for business development and productivity improvement

PRE-REFORM PERIOD & RRB

The 1981 report published by RBI about RRB's reveals that:

i) As far as loan policies are concerned, RRB's had followed instructions of the RBI as well as the Govt. of India

ii) RRB's served the rural economy by providing credit for productive activities

iii) But, RRB's recovery position was not satisfactory

PROBLEMS RECOVERY OF RRB's

Recovery of RRB's has varied between 51% to 61% and as a result overdues have varied between 39% to 49%.

Now Problems of recovery are of two types:

i) Internal problems include weak monitoring as well as supervision, improper use of loan & failure to link lending.

ii) External problems include political interference, willful default & effects of natural calamities.

The following are the recommendations of some committee both in the pre and post reform period which were formed by the government of India under the chairperson of various personalities. They are as follows:

Narsimham Committee

i) Commercial Banks should segregate the operations of their rural branches through formation of subsidiaries. Each rural subsidiary should operate on a compact area for proper supervision.

ii) Banks should have the freedom to swap rural branches.

iii) The rural subsidiaries should be treated at par with RRB's in regard to CRR & SLR.

iv) RRB's & their sponsoring banks should merge on voluntary basis.

Khusroo Committee

The RRB's had accumulated huge losses and they were named insolvent institutions and as a result they should be merged with the sponsoring banks for betterment of rural credit in the country.

M.C.Bhandari Committee

Thereafter the RBI appointed this committee for suggestions. The committee recommended that the issued share capital of RRB's should be enhanced from Rs 75 lakh to Rs 1 crore.

POST REFORM PERIOD & R.R.B

Vyas Committee

Merger should take place for RRBs in the same State. So, RRBs of the same sponsor bank should be merged at State-level. The number of RRBs was reduced as a result

Implementations so far:-

- **Widening network and Expanding coverage:**

  The objective of the RRB's is to cover all the districts of India because 87 districts are not yet covered.

- **Separate credit plan for excluded regions:**

  RRBs operating in predominantly tribal areas and having high levels of exclusion may prepare annual credit plans having a separate component for excluded groups, which would integrate credit provision with promotional assistance such as agricultural services for the farm and nonfarm sectors. Refinance and promotional support may be provided by NABARD to RRBs on a large scale for implementation of these credit plans.

- **NABARD to support HR development in RRBs:**

  RRBs has been serving with the support of NABARD, Govt. of India, RBI and the sponsor banks, as active financial inclusion players specially in areas with high levels of financial exclusion. In order to build up the skills and expertise of the personnel of RRBs, NABARD has played a crucial role. In addition NABARD was entrusted with the responsibility of coordination and Supervision of the selection process of employees in the RRBs. Local staff may be appointed as far as possible. With the help of local people RRB will be able to strengthen effective credit administration by way of credit appraisal, monitoring the progress of loans and their efficient recovery.

  Co-ordination between district level development planning and district level credit planning is also required in order to chart out the specific role of the RRB as a development agency of the rural areas.

- **Computerisation:**

  Computer support for banking transactions is needed & introduced.

- **Tax Incentives:**

  From 2006-07, RRBs are liable to pay income tax. To strengthen the RRBs, profits transferred to reserves could be exempted from tax till they achieve standard capital adequacy ratios. Alternately, RRBs may be allowed tax concessions to the extent of 40% of their profits, as per provisions under Sec. 36 (1) (viii) of the Income Tax Act. The aggregate CDR of RRBs increased over the years from 41.83% as on 31 March 2002 to 66.13% as on 31 March 2013. Nine of the RRBs reported CDR of more than 100%.

RRB's are going through a process of amalgamation and consolidation. 25 RRBs have been amalgamated in January 2013 into 10 RRBs. This counts 67 RRBs till the first week of June 2013. This counts 56 as of March 2015. On 31 March 2006, there were 133 RRBs (post-merger) covering 525 districts with a network of 14,494 branches. All RRBs were originally conceived as low cost institutions having a rural ethos, local feel and pro poor focus. However, within a very short time, most banks were making losses.

PRESENT SCENARIO

The following table-1 shows the number of banks in India in different areas along with the classification of the banks. Out of 97,473 branches of scheduled commercial banks conducting banking transactions in the country, out of which 35,966 (36.9%) bank branches are in the rural areas, 25,566 (26.2%) branches in urban areas, 18,694 ((19.17%) in semi-urban areas. It suggests that 63% of the total no. of branches are in rural and urban areas of the country.

Table-1: The number of banks in India in different areas along with the classification of the banks

Bank Group	Rural	Urban	Semi-Urban	Metropolitan	Total
Public Sector	22,146	1,7803	14,223	13,231	67,403
Private Sector	1,555	4,660	3,580	3,621	13,416
Foreign Banks	7	9	61	247	324
RRBs	12,258	3,094	830	148	16,330
Total	35,966	25,566	18,694	17,247	97,473

Source: Dept. of Financial Services, Ministry of Finance, GoI as on 30th June, 2012.

CONCLUSION

Due to multi agency control of the Central Government, State Government and the Sponsor bank the RRB's have suffered various problems regarding management and organisation. But the problems are taken care of as well as different measures were taken to solve the basic problem of recovery to reduce the amount of loss. Government of India have entrusted the RBI and NABARD for restructuring RRB. NABARD have suggested different policies that would be beneficial for the RRBs like permitting them to relocate some of their loss-making branches at agricultural produce centers (mandis). Now they are allowed to give loans to the non-priority groups for consumer durables and they are also allowed to upgrade their activities. One more thing RRBs should keep in mind that they should not confine their operations only in agricultural sector but for their growth they should also provide benefits to small entrepreneurs, village and cottage industries and small farmers. And they should establish proper co-ordination with other institutional financing agencies, co-operative banks, commercial banks and local participants to enhance their capability and exploit untapped rural market. Rural banks need to remove lack of transparency in their operation which leads to unequal relationship between banker and customer. Banking staff should interact more with their customers to overcome this problem. Banks should open their branches in areas where customers are not able to avail banking facilities due to underdeveloped transport and communication facilities. In this competitive era, RRBs have to concentrate on speedy, qualitative and secure banking services to retain existing customers and attract potential customers.

REFERENCES

1. Sundaram and Varshney -Banking and Financial System — Sultan Chand and Sons – 2005.
2. Mithani and Gordon- Banking and Financial System - –Himalaya Publishing House – 2005.
3. Dhanraj.N & R Sai kumar a review on regional rural banks of india: performance analysis with respect to telangana state—AIJRRLJSM—Vol-1-Issue-4,May, 2016.
4. Dept. of Financial Services, Ministry of finance, GOI report on RRBs as on 31st March, 2011
5. Velayudham, T. K., and Sankaranarayanan, V. (1990) "Regional Rural Banks and Rural Credit: Some Issues", Economic and Political Weekly, September 22, pp.2157-2164.
6. NABARD: Reports
7. RBI, Monthly Bulletins, Various issues

11

Problems & Prospects of RRBs in India: An Overview

Tanay Kumar Pal
Dhiren Pal

INTRODUCTION

Rural Population of India constitute about 80% of total population of the country . Most of the rural people suffer from a great deal of poverty as well as unemployment . They are subject to exploitation in credit market due to lack of adequate institutional credit . In 1969, All India Rural Credit Survey Committee recommended multi agency approach in providing rural credit requirement of rural people, a new category of institutional sources of rural credit emerged . This is what is known as Regional Rural Bank .

OBJECTIVES OF STUDY

The present study aims at the following :-

i. To study the concept and genesis of RRBs

ii. To highlight the role of RRBs as an agency of creating banking habits among rural people

iii. To list out the problems faced by RRBs.

iv. To offer suggestions for strengthening RRBs.

RESEARCH METHODOLOGY

The present paper depends on information already available from published reports of RBI, RRB, NABARD, books and journals and reports of Govt. of India. Various websites have also been used for preparation of this paper.

GENESIS OF RRBs

The establishment of Regional Rural Banks (RRBs) in India is a land mark in the banking history of India. The RRBs were established on 02 Oct. 1975 under the provision of the Regional Rural Banks Ordinance, 1975 promulgated by the Govt. of India on 26 Sept. 1975.

Initially, five RRBs were set up at Moradabad and Gorakhpur in Uttar Pradesh, Bhiwani in Haryana, Jaipur in Rajasthan and Malda in West Bengal. Each RRB has an authorized capital of Rs. I crore and issued capital of Rs. 25 lakh. Of the issued capital 50 percent is subscribed by the Govt. of India, 15 percent by the concerned State Govt. and the balance 35 percent by the sponsor bank.

The management of each RRB is vested in a nine member Board of Directors headed by a Chairman who is appointed by the Govt. of India. All the RRBs established in the country have been included in the second schedule to RBI Act, 1934.

The Govt. of India is the major shareholder (50%) and invented with powers to issue directives to RRBs, After the establishment of the NABARD in July, 1982, certain function such as statutory inspection of RRBs have been transferred from RBI to NABARD by amending Banking Regulation Act, 1949. However, other statutory functions relating to scheduling, cash reserve SLR requirement, branch licensing, etc remain with RBI. NABARD has also been overseeing the functioning of RRBs on behalf of Govt. of India and has also been issuing guidelines & instructions, wherever necessary, in consultation with the Govt. of India. NABARD is the regulatory body of RRBs.

The objective of setting up RRBs is to provide credit and other banking facilities especially to small and marginal farmers, agricultural laborers, artisans and small entrepreneurs in the rural areas. Each RRB works within local area specified by notification of the Govt. of India.

ROLE OF RRBs

Rural Banking is the process of conducting banking business in the rural economy where bank branches are too far away to be of use. The importance of rural banking in the economy development of a country cannot be overlooked. Mahatma Gandhiji said, Real India lies in villages develop village economy is the back bone of India. Without the development of rural economy, objectives of economic planning cannot be achieved. RBI in association with other commercial banks has taken various initiatives to build up a strong financial system (by offering versions loans) RRBs also, by doing general banking business, are logging a key rate in rural economy. In addition to general banking business, RRBs are also providing the following services for rural development).

Opening of no-frills account: RRBs are encouraging rural people to open up bank account with nil or minimum balance.

Relaxation on know your Customer (KYC) norms: Since August 2005, KYC requirements for opening bank accounts were relaxed for small accounts. RRBs are now permitted to take any evidence as to the identity and address of the customer to their satisfaction.

Business Correspondents: In 2006 RBI permitted banks to engage business facilitators (BFs) and business Correspondents (BCs) as intermediaries for providing doorstep financial & banking services.

General Credit Cards (GCC): With a view to helping the poor and needy people of the society banks are advised to provide access to easy credit upto a certain amount at their rural and semi-urban branches.

AMALGAMATION OF RRBs

RRBs were established as a new set of state-sponsored, rural-oriented, region-based and low cost banks having the ethos of Co-Operative banks and Commercial banks for providing credit in rural areas, particularly to the weaker section of the society. It is argued that RRBs have achieved a great success in providing rural credit to target groups.

However, RRBs faced burgeoning losses and became unviable because of some impediments in the process of banking business. Confronted with situation, Govt. of India were forced to start reform process. During a review carried out by GOI in 2009 it was found Capital Risk Weighted Assets Ratio (CRAR) of RRBs was too low. Therefore Dr. K.C. Chakraborty Committee suggested to bring CRAR to at 9 percent in a sustainable manner.

It was suggested by Agricultural Credit and Review Committee to make as amalgamation of unviable RRBs with sponsor bank for the creation of viable RRBs. Finally, it was decided to amalgamate some of the RRBs on grounds of contiguity in a particular region. The process of amalgamation has continued till June, 2014 and out of 196 RRBs in the year 2005, the number has been reduced to sixty four in March, 2013. And it has been 56 in July, 2014. The number of RRBs has decreased due to amalgamation as compared to other banks. The Growth of RRBs is shown in the table below.

Table-1: Growth of RRBs

Year	No. of Commercial Banks	Scheduled Commercial Banks excluding RRBs	RRBs	Non-scheduled Commercial Banks.
2005	288	88	196	4
2006	222	85	133	4
2007	183	83	96	4
2008	175	80	91	4
2009	170	80	86	4
2010	169	83	83	4
2011	169	83	82	4
2012	173	87	82	4
2013	155	87	64	4

Source : RBI Banking Report, 2013.

PROBLEMS & CHALLENGES OF RRBs

RRBs, so to say , had a rapid expansion of branch network and increase in the volume of banking business. Still RRBs are facing the following problems today.

1. RRBs are facing the problem of inadequate finance. They are to depend on NABARD to collect finance for their future operation. Poor rural people are unable to save anything due to poverty and low per capita income. The low level of saving of rural people creates an obstacle for RRBs to collect deposits.
2. High overdues and poor recovery of loan is one of the biggest concerns affecting the functioning of RRBs. The reasons for such high overdues and poor recovery are poor access of granting loans, untrained staff-unproductive or less productive use of credit, inadequate production, poor marketing facilities and improper channel of recovery system.
3. There is also a problem of regional imbalance in banking facilities provided by RRBs. This problem is created due to the concentration of bank branches in some specific regions and districts. As a result RRBs are losing other prospective customers.

4. May RRBs are suffering from the problem of heavy loans because of low repaying capacity of their customers , low level of deposits and heavy sanction of loan without considering the creditworthiness of the customers.
5. Lack of proper co-ordination between RRBs and other financial institutions like commercial banks NABARD and Co-operative banks has badly affected the performance of these banks.
6. RRBs have not still played a significant role in poverty alleviation of the country . Various efforts on the part of RRBs have been made but lack of economic infrastructure , poor knowledge of customers , low level of production , low awareness about savings have created many hurdles for RRBs.
7. Staff with low commitment to functional efficiency also adversely affect the working of RRBs.
8. Inadequate exposure and skills to innovate products are also limiting the lending portfolios of banks .

SUGGESTIONS

1. The state Govt. should take keen interest in the growth of RRBs.
2. RRBs may be permitted to lend up to 25% of their total advances to the richer section of the village society so that overdue may be reduced.
3. The unique role of RRBs in providing credit facilities to the weaker sections in the village must be preserved. RRBs should work as rural bank for the rural poor.
4. Local staff may be appointed as far as possible.
5. Participation of local people in the equity share capital of RRBs should be allowed and encouraged.
6. There should be a uniform pattern of interest rate structure for the rural financial agencies.
7. RRBs may relax their lending procedure and make them more easy for village borrowers.
8. Co-ordination between District level Development Planning and District Level Credit Planning is also required in order to chart out the specific role of RRB as a development agency of the rural areas.
9. RRBs may initiate certain new insurance policies like deposit-linked cattle and other animal insurance policies, crop insurance policies or life insurance policies for rural depositors.
10. RRBs must strengthen the credit administration system by way of credit appraisal, monitoring the progress of loans and their efficient recovery.
11. RRBs may join in consortium finance with public sector bank / Development financial institution (DFIs)

12. Securitization and Reconstruction of Financial Assets and Enforcement of Security Interest Act (SARFAESI) 2002 may be extended to RRBs.
13. RRBs may take up steps to constitute morel legal cells and tribunals , recovery branch , NPA management department etc for speedy recovery of NPAs in addition to existing methods .
14. Measures should be initiated to deploy credit to potential & productive sectors so that credit deployment may rise in proportion to deposits.

CONCLUSION

Today RRBs are facing a number of impediments in their holistic growth. To overcome there, RRBs should not only confine to agricultural sector but also provide banking services and other benefits to small entrepreneurs, village & cottage industries and small farmers. RRBs need to remove lack of transparency in their operation which lead to unequal relationship between banker and customer. And the RRBs should established proper co-ordination with co-operative banks. Commercial banks, other institutional agencies and local participant to enhance their capability. Besides, in this competitive era, RRBs have to concentrate on speedy, qualitative and secure banking services to retain existing customers and attract potential customers.

REFERENCES

1. Sharma K.C. – Modern Banking in India New Delhi, Deep & Deep Publications Pvt. Ltd. 2007.
2. Panandikar - Banking in India New Delhi Orient. Long man 1976.
3. Bose S. (2005) – The Regional Rural Banks : The past and Present Debate.
4. Kanan R. – (2004) – Regional Rural Banks.
5. Kothari C.R. – Research Methodology Methods and Technique (2008).
6. NABARD Annual Reports, 2009-11.
7. R.B.I. Monthly Bulletins.
8. Dept. of Financial Services, Ministry of Finance, GoI, Reports.
9. Devi. N.S. – Problems and Prospects of RRBs in India. IJMSR, Vol. – 2 April – 2004.
10. Dr. Subhra Gupta – Rural Financing (Role of RRBs) Kusukeshfra, June, 2011.
11. Websites.

12

Role of Regional Rural Bank in Financial Inclusion in India

Sk. Ataur Rahaman

INTRODUCTION

The genesis of the RRBs can be traced to the need for a stronger institutional arrangement for providing rural credit. The launch of regional rural banks (RRBs) can be seen as a unique experiment and experience in improving the efficacy of rural credit delivery mechanism in India. RRBs have been in existence for more than four decades with the objective of deepening the outreach of the banking system to serve specific population segments. From a modest beginning of 6 RRBs with 17 branches covering 12 districts in December 1975, their number grew into 57 RRBs (after amalgamation) in 2013-14 with 19,082 branches working in 642 districts across the country. The rural orientation of RRBs was formidable with rural and semi-urban branches constituting over 97 per cent of their branch network. The growth in the branch network enabled the RRBs to expand banking activities in the unbanked areas and mobilise rural savings. Thus RRBs have played a significant role in strengthening the banking network in India. However, despite all these efforts and the recent introduction of new Niche banks (that cater to and serve the needs of a certain demographic segment of the population), it could be challenged whether RRBs are playing the role for which they had been formed.

Now we will discuss RRBs' functions in respect of geographical periphery and their financial strength.

In this respect service coverage and the financial strength of RRBs are discussed in the following table.

Table-1: Shows service

Name of RRBs	States	Sponsor- bank	No. of RRBs	Total branches	Total funds (Rs in lac)	Total loan out-standing (Rs in lac)
Andhra Pradesh Grameena Vikas Bank	Andhra Pradesh	State Bank of India	8	638	260455.37	2026866.02
Andhra Pragathi Grameena Bank	Andhra Pradesh	Syndicate Bank	5	438		
Chaitanya Godavari Grameena Bank	Andhra Pradesh	Andhra Bank	3	128		
Deccan Grameena Bank	Andhra Pradesh	State Bank of Hyderabad	5	269		
Saptagiri Grameena Bank	Andhra Pradesh	Indian Bank	2	157		
Arunachal Pradesh Rural Bank	Arunachal Pradesh	State Bank of India	8	27	21581.95	6105.29
Assam Gramin Vikash Bank	Assam	United Bank of India	25	374	25399.28	843772.56
Langpi Dehangi Gramin Bank	Assam	State Bank of India	2	53		
Bihar Gramin Bank	Bihar	UCO Bank	9	243	112110.29	815504.60
Madhya Bihar Gramin Bank	Bihar	Punjab National Bank	11	474		
Uttar Bihar Gramin Bank	Bihar	Central Bank of India	18	1001		
Durg Rajnandgaon Gramin Bank	Chhatisgarh	Dena Bank	5	130	49204.05	205512.62
Surguja Kshetriya Gramin Bank	Chhatisgarh	Central Bank of India	4	103		
Chhattisgarh Gramin Bank	Chhattisgarh	State Bank of India	19	322		
Baroda Gujarat Gramin Bank	Gujarat	Bank of Baroda	12	151	42373.81	328083.50
Dena Gujarat Gramin Bank	Gujarat	Dena Bank	7	175		
Saurashtra Gramin Bank	Gujarat	State Bank of India	7	203		

Name of RRBs	States	Sponsor- bank	No. of RRBs	Total branches	Total funds (Rs in lac)	Total loan out-standing (Rs in lac)
Gurgaon Gramin Bank	Haryana	Syndicate Bank	7	231	108342.27	561391.34
Haryana Gramin Bank	Haryana	Punjab National Bank	16	276		
Himachal Pradesh Gramin Bank	Himachal Pradesh	Punjab National Bank	12	188	10275.28	89812.04
Ellaquai Dehati Bank	Jammu & Kashmir	State Bank of India	13	122	31302.00	120654.00
Jammu & Kashmir Grameen Bank	Jammu & Kashmir	Jammu & Kashmir Bank	13	201		
Jharkhand Gramin Bank	Jharkhand	Bank of India	15	239	27578.30	136211.13
Vananchal Gramin Bank	Jharkhand	State Bank of India	9	203		
Kaveri Grameena Bank	Karnataka	State Bank of Mysore	10	334	208982.07	1532187.24
Karnataka Vikas Grameena Bank	Karnataka	Syndicate Bank	9	524		
Krishna Grameena Bank	Karnataka	State Bank of India	3	168		
Pragathi Gramin Bank	Karnataka	Canara Bank	8	434		
North Malabar Gramin Bank	Kerala	Syndicate Bank	7	222	47094.42	756123.00
South Malabar Gramin Bank	Kerala	Canara Bank	8	284		
Narmada Jhabua Gramin Bank	Madhya Pradesh	Bank of India	13	313	119112.53	1126110.34
Madhyanchal gramin Bank	Madhya Pradesh	State Bank of India	12	396		
Central Madhya Pradesh Gramin Bank	Madhya Pradesh	Central Bank of India	25	423		
Maharashtra Gramin Bank	Maharashtra	Bank of Maharashtra	16	351	116210.23	1225112.62
Vidharbha Konkan Gramin Bank	Maharashtra	Bank of India	17	294		
Manipur Rural Bank	Manipur	United Bank Of India	9	28	3438.22	4567.96
Meghalaya Rural Bank	Meghalaya	State Bank of India	7	76	588.39	37885.27
Mizoram Rural Bank	Mizoram	State Bank of India	8	71	3289.18	53030.23

Name of RRBs	States	Sponsor- bank	No. of RRBs	Total branches	Total funds (Rs in lac)	Total loan out-standing (Rs in lac)
Nagaland Rural Bank	Nagaland	State Bank of India	5	10	1091.80	1872.09
Odisha Gramya Bank	Odisha	Indian Overseas Bank	13	475	97331.47	665413.01
Utkal Grameen Bank	Odisha	State Bank of India	17	426		
Puduvai Bharathiar Grama Bank	Puducherry	Indian Bank	2	30	2003.14	23777.74
Malwa Gramin Bank	Punjab	State Bank of Patialia	5	62	56977.81	419882.94
Punjab Gramin Bank	Punjab	Punjab National Bank	13	218		
Sutlej Gramin Bank	Punjab	Punjab & Sind Bank	6	31		
Mewar Aanchalik Gramin Bank	Rajastan	ICICI Bank Ltd	3	59	117256.67	938224.45
Baroda Rajasthan Kshetriya Gramin Bank	Rajasthan	Bank of Baroda	21	638		
Marudhara Gramin Bank	Rajasthan	State Bank of Bikaner & Jaipur	12	460		
Pallavan Grama Bank	Tamil Nadu	Indian Bank	15	150	69154.04	522229.84
Pandyan Grama Bank	Tamil Nadu	Indian Overseas Bank	16	224		
Tripura Gramin Bank	Tripura	United Bank Of India	8	133	27180.00	133822.68
Allahabad UP Gramin Bank	Uttar Pradesh	Allahabad Bank	11	555	411196.42	2308363.73
Aryavart Kshetriya Gramin Bank	Uttar Pradesh	Bank of India	9	406		
Ballia-Etawah Gramin Bank	Uttar Pradesh	Central Bank of India	4	143		
Baroda Uttar Pradesh Gramin Bank	Uttar Pradesh	Bank of Baroda	14	737		
Kashi Gomati Samyut Gramin Bank	Uttar Pradesh	Union Bank Of India	8	401		
Prathama Gramin Bank	Uttar Pradesh	Syndicate Bank	4	250		
Purvanchal Gramin Bank	Uttar Pradesh	State Bank of India	7	428		
Sarva UP Gramin Bank	Uttar Pradesh	Punjab National Bank	17	353		
Shreyas Gramin Bank	Uttar Pradesh	Canara Bank	7	245		

Name of RRBs	States	Sponsor- bank	No. of RRBs	Total branches	Total funds (Rs in lac)	Total loan out-standing (Rs in lac)
Uttarakhand Gramin Bank	Uttara-khand	State Bank of India	13	237	14819.55	130283.90
Bangiya Gramin Vikash Bank	West Bengal	United Bank of India	11	574	105740.22	500923.00
Paschim Banga Gramin Bank	West Bengal	UCO Bank	4	218		
Uttarbanga Kshetriya Gramin Bank	West Bengal	Central Bank of India	3	129		
Total			635	17,856		

Source NABARD (2014)

In the above table we see that the magnitude of service coverage of RRBs in India is very significant. Their service is spread over 26 states and in different names.

RECENT PERFORMANCE OF RRBs:

Within two decades of their existence, the RRBs had become financially weak and Government of India (GOI) initiated recapitalization of the RRBs along with several other policy initiatives to give them operational freedom for enhancing their business opportunities and profitability. Subsequently, in September, 2005, GOI initiated the first phase amalgamation of RRBs, sponsor bank-wise, at state level. By March, 2010, RRBs of the same sponsor banks within a State were amalgamated bringing down their number from 196 to 82. In the second and ongoing phase, starting from October, 2012, geographically contiguous RRBs within a State under different sponsor banks are being amalgamated to have just one RRB in medium-sized and two/three RRBs in large states. During the year 2013-14, 13 RRBs have been amalgamated into 6 new RRBs in 5 States (Chhattisgarh, Uttar Pradesh, Kerala, Karnataka and Haryana). With this, the effective number of RRBs as on 31st March, 2014 stands at 57 playing a significant role in developing agriculture and rural economy. *(DFS, 2015)*

RRBs generally work in difficult conditions-in semi-urban and rural areas–but with a low ticket size of product and with many regulatory constraints. Besides, RRBs are required to play a particular developmental role with stringent conditions are being placed on them in terms of priority sector lending norms. Thus their profitability is affected by serving scattered and less profitable clientele, with small loan sizes and other service delivery constraints.

Table-2: Comparative position of key performance indicators of RRB (Amt. in crore)

Years	2011-12	2012-13	2013-14 *	% Growth
Staff	74291	76246	80075	5.02
Owned Fund	16462	19445	22103	13.67
Deposit	186336	211488	239503	13.25
Borrowings	30289	38073	51208	34.50
Investments	95975	108548	110514	1.81
Gross Loan (O/s)	116385	139652	159302	14.07

Source: RBI-Annual Report

It is analysed in the above table that in respect of staff, owned funds deposits & borrowing, investment and gross loan outstanding the performance of RRBs is laudable. The growth of all parameters is strongly positive. Specially in terms of gross loan outstanding the growth is about 14per cent.

Now we will see the sector wise outstanding advances of RRBs in India.

Table-3: Purpose-wise Outstanding Advances by RRBs

Sl. No.	Purpose	(Rs. in Crore)		
	years	2011-12	2012-13	2013-14*
	Total loans outstanding	**1,16,385**	**1,39,652**	**1,59,302**
I	**Agriculture (i to iii)**	**63,823**	**75,200**	**90,294**
(a)	Short term loans (crop loans)	46,580	55,255	68,267
(b)	Term loans (for agriculture and allied)	17,244	19,406	21,952
II	**Non-agriculture (i to iv)**	**52,561**	**64,452**	**79,008**
(a)	Share of agriculture to total loans o/s	54.84	53.84	56.68
(b)	Share of term loans to total loans o/s	14.81	13.89	13.78
III	**Priority Sector**			
(a)	Priority Sector	95542	111812	130215
(b)	Non-Priority Sector	20843	25266	29087
	Share of Priority Sector (% to total)	**82.09**	**80.06**	**81.74**

* Provisional: Source: DFS (2015)

From table-3 it is seen that there has been a steady increase in the total advances outstanding of RRBs over the past three years, with the figure increasing from Rs.1,16,385 crore to Rs. 1,59,302 crore. It is also seen in respect of purpose-wise outstanding advances by RRBs in India that the share of agriculture is around 57 per cent and the growth of which is about 20 per cent. The predominant form of loan to agriculture is the short-term or crop loan, with the share of term loans to agriculture accounting for around 14 per cent. The share of priority Sector advances which stood at 80.06 per cent of the total outstanding advances of RRBs as on 31st March, 2013 has increased to 81.74 per cent as on 31st March, 2014. The share of agricultural loans increased from 53.84 per cent as on 31st March, 2013 to 56.68 per cent as on 31st March, 2014.

The total credit flow to agriculture (agency-wise) during the last three years period by all agencies is as under.

Table-4: Credit flow to agriculture by RRBs in comparison to commercial banks (Amt. Rs. in crore)

Year	2011-12	2012-13	2013-14 *
SCARDBs	2,410	1,554	1,869
% share to total	0.5	0.3	0.2
STCBs	85,553	1,09,649	1,18,095
% share to total	**16.7**	**18.1**	**16.6**
RRBs	**54,450**	**63,681**	**82,653**
% share to total	**10.7**	**10.5**	**11.6**
Commercial Banks	3,68,616	4,32,491	5,09,005
% share to total	72.1	71.2	71.5
Total	**5,11,029**	**6,07,376**	**7,11,622**

From Table-4 we see that the total credit flow to agriculture i.e. ground level credit is more or less intact during last three years. In respect of commercial bank it is also unchanged.

Loan disbursement of RRBs to small /marginal farmers during 2011 to 2014 is shown below.

Table-5: Loan disbursed by RRBs to small /marginal farmers in comparison to commercial banks (No. Rs. in lakh and Rs. in crore)

Sl. No.	Agencies	No. of A/C	Disbursement	Of which A/Cs pertaining to SF/MF	% share to total number of A/Cs	Of which Credit disbursed to SF/MF	% share to total credit disbursed
I	Comm. Banks	379.04	5,09,004.96	234.52	61.87	2,01,296.26	39.55
II	Coop. Banks	321.37	1,19,963.79	206.05	64.12	69,352.24	57.81
III	RRBs	99.27	82,652.72	66.62	67.11	51,358.81	62.14
Total	**799.68**	**7,11,621.47**	**507.19**	**63.42**	**3,22,007.31**	**45.25**	

From Table-5 it is seen that RRBs had the highest share of disbursement to small and marginal farmers both in terms of number and amount disbursed among all the agencies during 2013-14.

NABARD officials assert that RRBs are the true microfinance institutions. Out of a total outstanding of Rs. 1,59,000 crore, Rs. 82,000 crore is the ground level disbursement. 61% of clients are small and marginal farmers: in commercial banks, this percentage is only 39%. RRBs are filling the gaps which commercial banks are not able to cover.

RRBs' LATEST ACHIEVEMENT IN FINANCIAL INCLUSION

Measures and products designed to reach the unbanked and the poor have been advocated and consciously implemented for decades. The RBI perception appears to be that financial inclusion is largely a matter related to banks' initiatives rather than the concern of a wider range of players in microfinance covering PACS, MFIs, SHGs, etc. Consequently the financial inclusion discourse has focused on bank-level products and initiatives and the corresponding targets. The two planks of the commercial banks' involvement in the larger financial inclusion project have been (i) avenues for outsourcing through different types of agent structures and (ii) the introduction of IT-based devices and innovations for low-cost operations and for accounting and MIS. In fact, the current financial inclusion campaign has been positioned as a kind of successor to the (less than successful) earlier attempts at inclusive finance through RRBs, SHGs, etc. The approach to RRB reform (of recapitalisation and amalgamation) too had been seen as one which was politically pragmatic characterised by an indifference towards the financial inclusion objective of RRB operations (MCril, 2008). Nevertheless it was also observed that despite the apparent importance of commercial banks even in the rural areas however they were neither able nor willing to serve the poorest sections of the population. By comparison, in the credit categories of direct relevance to financial inclusion, RRBs held over a quarter of agricultural credit accounts and over half of all artisan/tiny industry loan accounts with barely 11% respectively in the total credit for these two categories. It also showed that RRBs had a far higher proportion of small loan accounts than other types of banks.

In similar vein, the Annual Report 2013–14 of RBI (RBI, 2014) has stated that microfinance institutions and small RRBs can certainly help in furthering access to finance. However, they cannot on their own bridge the gaps. Well-capitalized and robust financial institutions are needed to take up the financial inclusion agenda.

The Swabhimaan programme launched by the Ministry of Finance, Government of India and the India Banks' Association (IBA) aimed to bring banking within the reach of the masses through brick and mortar branches or through various forms of ICT-based models including through business correspondents (BCs). All public and private sector banks were advised to draw a three-year financial inclusion plan (FIP) starting from April 2010, duly approved by their Board and with related business plans. The spectacular growth numbers in the parameters being tracked by FIPs would appear to suggest that the financial inclusion project is on track in terms of achievements and initiatives aimed at financial inclusion. Banks have made notable, sporadic, efforts at innovation in support in the introduction of technology, financial literacy and other methods of expanding outreach, with RRBs too contributing in equal measure.

The Committee set up by the RBI, states that "the essence of financial inclusion is in trying to ensure that a range of appropriate financial services is available to every individual and enabling them to understand and access those services. Apart from the regular form of financial intermediation, it may include a basic no frills banking account for making and receiving payments, a savings product suited to the pattern of cash flows of a poor household, money transfer facilities, small loans and overdrafts for productive, personal and other purposes, etc. In this they have been supported by NABARD through the Financial Inclusion Fund (FIF) and the Financial Inclusion and Technology Fund (FITF). FIF meets the cost of developmental and promotional interventions and FITF meets the cost of technology adoption for financial inclusion. As on 31 March 2014 cumulative disbursements were Rs. 135.35 crore under the FIF and Rs. 221.55 crore under FITF.

The experience of the FIFs to increase outreach to an increasing large number of villages and unserved areas have led to the Pradhan Mantri

Jan-Dhan Yojana (PMJDY) launched in 2014. According to the PMJDY Mission document, though the banks achieved their targets under the first phase of the Swabhimaan campaign, it had very limited reach and impact. Public Sector Banks (PSBs) including RRBs estimated that by 31 May 2014, out of the 131.4 million rural households which were allocated to them for coverage, about 59.4 million remained uncovered. Comprehensive financial inclusion (FI) under the mission is based on six pillars of achievement with well-defined targets.

Table 6: Pradhan Mantri Jan-Dhan Yojana (Accounts opened till 15.07.2015) (Rs.in crore)

Sl. No.		No. of Accounts			No. of Rupay debit	Balance in A/C	% of Zero balance
		Rural	Urban	Total			
1	Public Sector Banks	7.24	5.98	13.22	12.25	15,698.68	50.83
2	Regional Rural	2.57	0.44	3.02	2.19	3,493.76	50
3	Private Banks	0.41	0.28	0.69	0.61	1,095.93	47.83
	Total	10.21	6.71	16.92	15.05	20,288.37	50.59

Source: DFS, GOI.

Table-6 shows RRB achievements under the new financial inclusion strategy. It shows the number of accounts opened under the PMJDY as on 15.07.2015. An indicator of participation in financial inclusion efforts currently is the number of accounts opened under the PMJDY. RRBs opened 3.02 crore accounts under PMJDY, as on 15.07.2015, or nearly 18 per cent of total accounts. Public sector banks opened 13.22 crore accounts and private banks 0.69 crore accounts. RRBs accounted for 2.57 crore accounts in rural areas opened under the PMJDY up to 15.07.2015. This represents over 25 per cent of the total 10.21 crores accounts opened in rural areas. RRBs accounted for nearly Rs. 3,500 crores out of Rs. 20,288 crores of deposits, representing over 17 per cent of the balances in these accounts. The percentage of zero balance accounts out of these newly opened accounts is 50 per cent. RRBs have also opened 4, 40,000 accounts in urban areas.

Public sector banks issued 12.25 crore RuPay debit cards and private banks 0.61 crore such cards. The number of RuPay debit cards issued by RRBs was 2.19 crores, out of a total number of 15.05 crore such cards issued by all types of banks.

Apart from the accounts opened under PMJDY and savings deposited by RRBs, they have accounted for a large number of initiatives in terms of products offered and infrastructure support provided towards financial inclusion. The range of such products is large and varies from RRB to RRB. It includes various types of deposit accounts and credit/debit smart cards, insurance products, financial literacy initiatives, Direct/Electronic Benefit Transfers (DBT and EBTs), pensions and various types of loan initiatives such as housing, education. These products have been deployed through various types of outlets, which include brick and mortar branches, Customer Service Point (CSP) outlets, kiosk banking, ultra small branches (USBs), with the help of ATMs and tablet-based micro ATMs and Point of Sale (POS) devices.

As per NABARD sources, in terms of Financial Inclusion, RRBs are playing a major role. All RRBs have migrated to the Core Banking Solution platform–for which NABARD by supporting 28 loss-making banks has played a pivotal role. Also they have, at par with other banks, taken up RTGS and have been supported for deploying ATMs for banking and financial services in North-East region. All RRBs have signed a MOU for implementing Jan Suraksha Yojana and Jeevan Jyoti Yojana. They have issued smart cards of various types and generally have been at the forefront of the financial inclusion measures.

However, this rapid expansion of the banking and financial infrastructure has not been without cost. The opening of new accounts and building the physical and human infrastructure for the financial inclusion mission has been undertaken on a war footing without regard to the initial costs and necessary maintenance costs. The expenditure on opening and servicing over three crore new accounts under the financial inclusion drive–even though half of them may not yet be operational–is quite substantial and goes beyond the call of the RRBs functions and immediate objectives. It would be instructive to examine whether the RRBs load of JDY and financial inclusion efforts.

CONCLUDING OBSERVATIONS AND SUGGESTIONS

As the majority of the rural population is still not included in the inclusive growth, the concept of financial inclusion becomes a challenge for the Indian economy. Since 2005, many concerted measures are initiated by the Reserve Bank of India and Government of India in favor of financial inclusion but the impact of these did not yield satisfactory results as a whole. In this perspective the role of RRBs in financial inclusion in India is not so disheartening. They have played a key role in rural institutional financing in terms of geographical coverage, clientele outreach and business volume as also contribution to development of the rural economy. However, as new entities are being created particularly in the rural banking space there appears to be a potential surge in the availability of financial services to medium scale enterprises and middle income groups which too have probably not received their fair quantum of services over the years. Specially in respect performance of the RRBs in financial inclusion some major issues are needed to be addressed like financial mechanism in the emergence of private player, scale up the original mandate, viability and profitability, source of investment fund, efficient use of human resource and technology etc. So, this will require sustained support from the sponsor banks, RBI and NABARD to mitigate these challenges and thereby to strengthen the role of RRBs in financial inclusion.

REFERENCES

- Government of India, Department of Financial Services, (2015), "Consolidated Review of Performance of Regional Rural Banks", http://financialservices.gov.in/banking/Consolidated%20Review%20RRB.
- Malhotra, Rakesh (2003), "Performance of RRBs: Effect of umbilical cord", published in Bank Quest", Journal of Indian Institute of Bankers, Vol. 74, No.1, January-March.
- Misra, Biswa Swarup (2006), "The Performance of Regional Rural Banks (RRBs) in India: Has Past Anything to Suggest for Future?", Reserve Bank of India Occasional Papers, Vol. 27, No. 1 and 2, Summer and Monsoon.
- NABARD, 2014, "Study on Viability of Business Correspondents in Regional Rural Banks", NABARD-Mumbai, June 30.
- Reserve Bank of India (2014), Financial Stability Report, (including Trend and Progress in Banking in India 2013-14), Issue no. 10, December.

13

Role of Regional Rural Banks on Rural Development :
A Study of Awareness of Students with special reference to few Colleges in Paschim Medinipur District, West Bengal, India

Pankaj Kumar Paul

INTRODUCTION

The nationalization of the banks boosted the confidence of the public in the Banking system of the country in 1969. However, in the early 1970s, there was a feeling that even after nationalization, there were cultural issues which made it difficult for commercial banks, even under government ownership, to lend to farmers. This issue was taken up by the government and it set up Narasimham Working Group in 1975. Regional Rural Banks (RRBs) came into existence on Gandhi Jayanti (2nd October) in 1975 associated with the initial name as *Prathama Grameen Bank*. The rural banks had the legislative backing of the Regional Rural Banks Act 1976. This act allowed the government to set up banks from time to time wherever it considered necessary (Garhwal, 1993; Gupta, 1987; Kapoor, 2004). Regional Rural Banks were conceived as low cost institutions having a rural ethos, local feel and pro poor focus. Every bank was to be sponsored by a "Public Sector Bank", however, they were planned as the self sustaining credit institution which were able to refinance their internal resources in themselves. The RRBs were owned by the Central Government, the State Government and the Sponsor Bank (Five commercial banks - Punjab National Bank, State Bank of India, Syndicate Bank, United Bank of India and United Commercial Bank, which sponsored the RRBs) who held shares in the ratios as follows - Central Government-50%, State Government- 15% and Sponsor Banks-35% (Singh, 1992; Chandrasekhar, 1985).

OBJECTIVES OF THE STUDY

Following objectives are laid down to substantiate the present study:

1. To study role of RRBs on rural development in India;
2. To analyse the gender discrepancy in opinion among the students;
3. To examine the impact of selected indicators associated with the successfulness of RRBs on rural development;
4. To examine the attitudinal differences in awareness among the students towards the impact of RRBs on rural development w.r.t. gender, location and socio-economic status.

Hypotheses

The study tested the following hypotheses:

$^0H_1$: There is no gender discrepancy in opinion among the students regarding the role of RRBs on rural development;

$^0H_2$: There are no attitudinal differences about awareness towards the impact of RRBs on rural development of the students belonging to male and female category;

$^0H_3$: There are no attitudinal differences about awareness towards the impact of RRBs on rural development of the students residing in rural or urban areas;

$^0H_4$: There are no attitudinal differences about awareness towards the impact of RRBs on rural development of the students belonging to APL and BPL.

MATERIALS AND METHODS OF THE STUDY

Materials

This study is empirical in nature. A self-made structured questionnaire has been used to collect the primary data from twenty colleges of 710 students of Paschim Medinipur district in West Bengal in 2015-16.

Methods

The following statistical methods have been used to analyse the present study:

1. Chi-square test to examine the gender discrepancy in opinion among the students;
2. Binary logit regression model to examine the relationship between RRBs and rural development with a set of selected indicators associated.
3. Student's t-test to examine the differences in attitude about awareness towards the impact of RRBs on rural development among the respondents w.r.t. location, socio-economic status and gender.

ANALYSIS AND DISCUSSION

Significance of the gender difference in the opinion of the respondents about association between RRBs and Rural Development

The opinions of the respondents about the association between RRBs and rural development is shown in table 1.

Table–1: Particulars regarding the opinion of the respondents about association between RRBs and Rural Development

Respondents	Yes	Uncertain	No	Total	Value of χ^2	Level of significance
Boys'	315	30	15	360		
Girls'	320	20	10	350		
Total	635	50	25	710	3.83	P>0.05 (Not significant)

Source: Field Survey, 2013-14

It appears from table-1 that the calculated value of chi-square is less than the tabulated value both at 5% and 1% level of significance. Therefore, the null hypothesis (i.e., ${}^{0}H_{1}$) is accepted indicating that there is no gender discrepancy in opinion among the students regarding the role of RRBs on rural development.

Promotion of humanistic Education: A Binary Logit Regression Model

Table-2: Showing Binay Logit Analysis explaining scope of Rural Development through RRBs

$SRRD = C_0 + C_1 * PBH + C_2 * MS + C_3 *GEL + C_4 *EEA + C_5 *DRI + C*_6 DC$				
Indicators	Coefficient	Std. Error	Z-Stat	Prob.
C	11.61421	3.671901	5.231567	0.0000*
Promotion of Banking Habits (PBH)	0.089632	0.415623	3.167541	0.0020*
Mobilisation of Savings (MS)	2.631290	0.719820	4.432705	0.0000*
Granting Education Loan (GEL))	0.642318	0.167261	0.376516	0.0000*
Expansion of Economic Activities (EEA)	1.416743	0.914230	0.512802	0.0000*
Development of Rural Infrastructure (DRI)	0.853601	0.511782	4.412380	0.0231*
Diversification Consumption (DC)	2.152640	0.715429	4.451287	0.6301**

Source: Authors' calculation based on field survey, 2015-16

Note:(i) Dependent Variable = Successfulness of RRBs in Rural Development (SRRD)

(ii) Total number of Respondents (N) = 710

(iii) * = Significant and ** = Insignificant

It is revealed from the results (vide table 2) that the indicators - PBH, MS, GEL, EEL, DRI and DC are positively associated with the successfulness of rural development of RRBs. Again these indicators are observed to be significant to rural development about RRBs with the exception of one indicator i.e., DC since it suffers from the problem of insignificancy. This indicates a question mark about awareness among the respondents regarding consumption expenditure in term of consumption loan taken from the RRBs.

Significance in difference in the mean scores of attitude of the respondents about awareness towards the impact of RRBs on Rural Development

Table -3: Showing the 't' value between mean scores of attitude about awareness of students towards impact of RRBs on rural development in male and female category

Gender	N	M	SD	SE_D	t	Level of significance
Boys'	360	67.51	6.87	0.53	3.91	0.01
Girls'	350	65.43	7.32			

Source: Authors' calculation based on field survey, 2015-16

Table 3 indicates that the value of 't' between mean scores of attitudes of students in boys and girls towards the impact of RRBs on rural development is statistically significant at 0.01 level. Therefore this result leads to conclude that the awareness of boys and girls students towards the impact of RRBs on rural development differ significantly. So the hypothesis-$^0H_2$ is rejected.

Table-4: Showing the 't' value between mean scores of attitude about awareness of students towards impact of RRBs on rural development residing in urban and rural areas

Residing area	N	M	SD	SE_D	t	Level of significance
Urban	310	84.62	7.30			
Rural	400	61.38	8.41	0.60	38.65	0.01

Source: Authors' calculation based on field survey, 2015-16

Table 4 reveals that the value of 't' between mean scores of attitudes of students in rural and urban areas towards impact of RRBs on rural development is significant at 0.01 level. Therefore the result leads to conclude that the awareness of rural and urban students towards impact of RRBs on rural development differs significantly. So the hypothesis $^0H_3$ is rejected.

Table -5: Showing the 't' value between mean scores of attitude about awareness of students towards impact of RRBs on rural development belonging in APL and BPL

Economic status	N	M	SD	SE_D	t	Level of significance
APL	340	68.92	6.94			
BPL	370	66.43	5.37	0.46	5.37	0.01

Source: Authors' calculation based on field survey, 2015-16

N.B. APL = Above Poverty Line

BPL = Below Poverty Line

Table 3 point out that the value of 't' between mean awareness scores of attitudes of students comprising in APL and BPL groups towards the impact of RRBs on rural development is significant at 0.01 level. Thus the result leads to the conclusion that the awareness of APL and BPL students towards the impact of RRBs on rural development differ significantly. So the hypothesis-$^{0}H_5$ is rejected.

CONCLUDING REMARKS

This article describes the awareness of students about role of RRBs on rural development with special reference to few colleges of Paschim Medinipur district in West Bengal. The results exposed a significant relationship between RRBs and rural development in the study area. No gender discrepancy has been found regarding the opinion about role of RRBs on rural development. It is to be noted that there exists significant variation in attitudes about the awareness towards the role of RRBs on rural development among the students in the surveyed colleges according to gender, residing place and socio-economic status.

POLICY RECOMMENDATIONS

The following suggestions are made for successfulness of RRBs :

1. Commercial motivation of the clients;
2. Self-sustaining credit policy;
3. Credit –deposit ratio should be increased;
4. Exploring new avenues of investment;
5. Merger with the sponsored banks.

REFERENCES

- Chandrasekhar, K., (1985). 'History of Indian Banking', edited by Subrahmanya, S., Trends and progress of Banking in India, Deep and Deep Publications, New Delhi, p.13.
- Garhwal, S., (1993). 'Commercial Banking and Economic Development', Pointer Publishers, Jaipur-3.
- http://www.gktoday.in/blog/regional-rural-banks
- Gupta, S.C., (1987). 'Repayment Performance', Development Banking for Rural Development, Deep & Deep Publications, New Delhi-110027.
- Kapoor, G.P., (2004). 'Commercial Banking', A.P.H. Publishing Corporation, New Delhi.
- Singh, Ajit (1992). 'Rural Development and Banking in India,. Theory and Practice', Deep and Deep Publications, New. Delhi 27.

14

Role of Regional Rural Banks in Microfinance: A Comparative Study of Two Districts of West Bengal

Ratul Saha
Bhajan Chandra Barman
Arun Kumar Roy

INTRODUCTION

Economic growth follows financial inclusion. In order to achieve the objective of growth with equity, it is imperative that infrastructure is developed with financial inclusion. In the recent times Government of India and financial regulators have taken several steps towards financial inclusion for achieving inclusive development. Among them microfinance approach is one whose primary aim is to bring the disadvantageous section of people under the purview of the formal financial institutions. In developing economies, the banks, as mobilisers of savings and allocators of credit for production and investment, have a very critical role. As a financial intermediary, the banks contribute to the economic growth of the country. However, it is disheartening to note that the number of people with access to the products and services offered by the banking system continues to be very limited even years after introduction of inclusive banking initiatives in the country through measures such as the cooperative movement, nationalization of banks, creation of regional rural banks, etc. Banks used to serve mainly the richer rural borrowers, not the ones who have nothing to give as collaterals. Over the past five years, the Reserve Bank of India and other policy makers have given a deep attention to the financial inclusion and achieved discernible progress in improving access to financial services for the masses.

However, the progress is far from satisfactory as evidenced by the World Bank Survey (2012). According to the survey findings, only 35 per cent of Indian adults had access to a formal bank account. Only 2 per cent of adults used an account to receive payment from a family member living in another area. NSSO data reveal that 45.9 million farmer households in the country (51.4%), out of a total of 89.3 million households do not access credit, either from institutional or non-institutional sources. Further, despite the vast network of bank branches, only 27% of total farm households are indebted to formal sources.

Under the above circumstances microfinance has emerged as a powerful tool for easy access to financial inclusion to the rural needy poor, specially the rural women. Credit goes to Md Yunus who first pave the way by showing that the poor are also credit worthy through his research project in the year 1976. His financial institution Grameen Bank in Bangladesh starts with a small amount of money worth of $27and providing this amount to a group of 42 families with the view that these families would create small items related to our everyday life for sale. Now it is a history that by 2006 the bank branches are numbered over 2100 and its success inspired more than 40 countries across the world. At present it becomes a model of the World Bank. It has been proved by Prof. Yunus that the poor are indeed efficient enough to manage credit and repay loans in due time with due interest. Experience of different anti-poverty and other welfare programmes within the country and elsewhere have shown that the key to its success lies in the participation of community based organizations at the grassroots level. People's participation in credit delivery, recovery and linking of formal credit institutions to borrowers through the intermediation of self-help groups (SHGs) have been recognized as a supplementary mechanism for providing credit support to the rural poor. In the present paper we have tried to make a comparative analysis of the physical and financial performance of the RRBs in CoochBehar and Bankura districts of West Bengal under SGSY with the help of number of self help groups formed, Gradation pattern, savings linkage, credit linkage and project linkage self help groups during the period 2009 to 2013.

Large numbers of studies have been made internationally as well as nationally on the working of the micro finance and of the self help groups in this regard. We oblige to mention selectively some of them in the following paragraphs.

Amin and Pebley (1994) in reviewing gender inequality within households have observed that BRAC's loan contributed to increase women's mobility outside the home and their control on household resources and household decision making power. They also revealed that the incidence of abandonment reduces with the receiving of micro-credit loans.

Jai (1996) in his study analyzed the role of RRBs in Economic Development and revealed that RRBs played a vital role in the field of rural development. Moreover, RRBs were more efficient in disbursal of loans to the rural borrowers as compared to the commercial banks. Support from the State Governments, local participation, and proper supervision of loans and opening urban branches were some steps recommended to make RRBs further efficient.

Mayoux (1997) points out that the impact of microfinance on women varies from woman to woman. These differences arise due to the difference in productive activities or different background. Sometimes, microfinance mainly benefit the women who are already better off, whereas the poor women are either neglected by the microfinance programmes or are least able to benefit because of their low resource base, lack of skills and market contacts. However, poorer women can also be more free and motivated to use credit for production.

Kumaran (1997) has made a case study of three SHGs, viz. active, passive and dissolved in Andhra Pradesh and found that the main factors responsible for active functioning of SHGs were solidarity and cohesiveness. On the other hand, passivity and dissolved were mainly on account of irregularities in savings and repayment of loan and lack of mutual trust and confidence among the members.

Zaman (2001) by assessing the poverty and vulnerability impacts of micro finance in Bangladesh comes to the conclusion that, SHGs play significant roles in reducing the vulnerability of the poor through income and consumption smoothing.

Satish (2001) in his paper raised some issues related to the functioning of SHGs. He has opined that adequate care should be taken to ensure homogeneity of socio-economic status of the member while forming SHGs. He suggested that SHG movement has to be spread all over rural India rather than being concentrated in a few pockets of the country.

Jayaraman (2002) shows very clearly after reviewing the performance of fisher women under different SHGs they are performing very well in availing, utilizing and repaying of micro-credit in time. Not only this study also reveals that this kind of SHG activities also reduces usury and elicit liquor in their society.

Myrada (2002) conducted an impact study among 190 members of 12 SHGs spread over Andhra Pradesh, Karnataka, Kerala and Tamil Nadu and find that relatively older groups have succeeded to increase their share in family income than those who are in younger groups. This is also true in the case of awareness about health and hygiene.

Sundar and Asokan (2004) in their paper focused the regional variations in implementation of women development programmes under SHG approach. They found that there is wide spread regional variation in implementation of women development programme in different parts of the country. Hence removal of regional variation in the performance of development programme depends on effective implementation of women development programmes.

Sen (2005) has made a study on the SHGs in West Bengal and found that the dependence on the internal resources is quite high because of the weak or inadequate bank linkage. The author also found that most of the poor households are ignorant of basic services and programmes to which they are entitled. Lack of intensive facilitation is the stumbling block. The author reports the lack of capacity building initiative without which the basic objective of the SHGs cannot be achieved.

Tessie Swope (2005) after a brief discussion in an independent study on micro-finance pointed out five main criticisms against it. They are: it does not reach to the poorest members of a population, it is not financially sustainable for institutions, it is potentially harmful to women (husbands zealous), it can create large debt for the poor and it is not universal in application.

Loganathan and Asokan (2006) in their study pointed out that there are vast variations in development of SHGs among the states and among the regions. Among the regions, southern region is the best region in financing SHGs. Next to that the performance of central region, eastern region and western region is moderate. The northern and north east regions are comparatively poor in financing SHGs.

Soundarapandian (2006) made an attempt in his article to analyze the growth of SHGs and the role of micro finance in developing the rural entrepreneurship. The study suggests that though there is a positive growth rate of SHGs in states but in terms of the growth of SHGs there is a wide variation among the states.

STUDY DESIGN

The first section of this write-up covers the introduction. Our second section deals with the objectives of the study, Research Methodology and study area. The third section presents a short overview of the status of the Self-Help Groups in West Bengal. In section four we discuss about the Physical Growth and Physical performance of SHGs in our study districts CoochBehar and Bankura. In section five we make a critical assessment of Financial Performance of the SHGs in the said districts. Finally we try to give some findings and concluding remarks in sixth section of this write-up.

OBJECTIVES OF THE STUDY

1. To measure the workability of the RRBs in the field of micro-finance and SHGs under SGSY in the proposed area.
2. To assess the variation in physical and financial achievements of the RRBs regarding microfinance activities among the districts of West Bengal.
3. To ascertain how far the physical growth of SHGs is associated with the financial achievement of the groups.
4. To make a comparison of the growth of SHG movement under SGSY in the two selected regions of West Bengal.

METHODOLOGY OF THE STUDY

This study is based on the secondary data and literature. Secondary data have been collected from various sources like District Rural Development Cells, Panchayat and Rural Development Department, Government of West Bengal, Census Report 2011 and various articles published in journals. A very simple mathematical tool has been used for the presentation of the data. Simple Bar diagrams have been used to represent the data graphically. For the purpose of the study two districts have been selected from the rural economy of West Bengal applying purposive sampling procedure. These two districts are Cooch Behar and Bankura. The selection of the two districts has been made because of the fact that these two districts are backward districts as per our census definition. Another reason is the geographical location of these two districts. The district Cooch Behar is located at the northern portion of our state while the other district Bankura is situated in the southern portion of the state economy of West Bengal. Locations of the sample districts in India as well as in West Bengal are given in Map I.

Map I

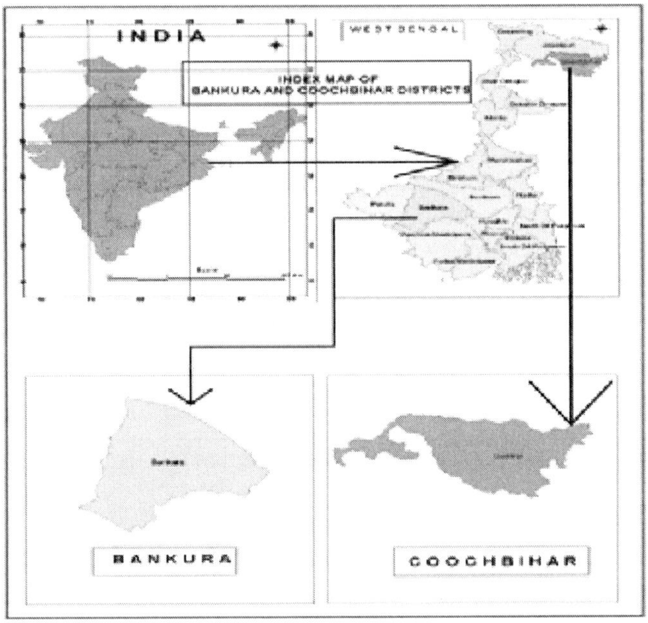

STATUS OF SHGs UNDER SGSY IN WEST BENGAL

In India, a number of SHGs were created in the 1980s for providing credit facilities to the poor, especially women, in both urban and rural areas. These SHGs stumbled upon a surprising finding: by targeting women, repayment rates came in well over 95 percent, higher than most traditional banks. Impressed by those repayment rates, institutions like National Bank for Agriculture and Rural Development (NABARD) and Small Industries Development Bank of India (SIDBI) began increasing their lending to SHGs in India. Government of India also to provide sustainable income to poor people living in rural areas of the country has launched Swarnajayanti Gram Swarojgar Yojana (SGSY) on April 1, 1999. The SGSY programme, in the line of NABARDS's SHG-bank Linkage programme, intended to extend micro-finance services to rural poor belonging to the socially and economically backward classes and the tribal population particularly in the economically backward regions, who are largely dependent on money lenders for meeting their emergent credit requirement for food, shelter and social ceremonies The District Rural Development Cell (DRDC) has been authorized to encourage the rural people to form SHGs and to supervise the working of these SHGs.

In Table 1, we rank the SHGs formed in different districts up to the year 2013by all the banks in the respective districts. As per our ranking Murshidabad becomes the top of the list followed by Midnapur West. Cooch Behar and Bankura rank respectively 9th and 11th position. All are also given in figure 1 to visualize the SHG formation. We also calculate the rate of growth of the SHGs in our study State considering 2009 as base year. During the reference period the average growth rate of the State becomes 46.84. We have find that 8 districts of our State record the growth rates which are above the State growth rates. The highest growth rate has been captured by the district 24 Pargana (South) followed by the Hoogly district. Our two Sub-Samples recorded 88.87 and 48.88 percentages of growth rates during the same reference period.

Table-1: District-wise Physical Progress of SHGs under SGSY in West Bengal

Sl. No.	District/State	No. of SHGs formed up to march 2013 by all Banks	Rank(R)	Percent Growth (2009-2013)
1	24 Parganas(N)	24252	6	58.32
2	24 Parganas(S)	33509	3	139.08
3	Bankura	21408	11	48.88
4	Birbhum	24512	5	43.55
5	Burdwan	23931	8	40.82
6	Coochbehar	23692	9	88.87
7	Darjeeling	8730	18	58.18
8	Dinajpur (S)	11033	17	13.20
9	Dinajpur (N)	12833	15	24.26
10	Hoogly	15328	14	124.88
11	Howrah	11063	16	60.89
12	Jalpaiguri	25600	4	19.38
13	Maldah	20207	13	31.09
14	Murshidabad	40855	1	41.37
15	Medinipur (E)	23906	7	35.12
16	Medinipur (W)	37819	2	36.03
17	Nadia	20765	12	63.13
18	Purulia	22528	10	11.80
State	West Bengal	401971	---------	46.84

Source: Panchayat & Rural Development Department, WB.

Fig.-1

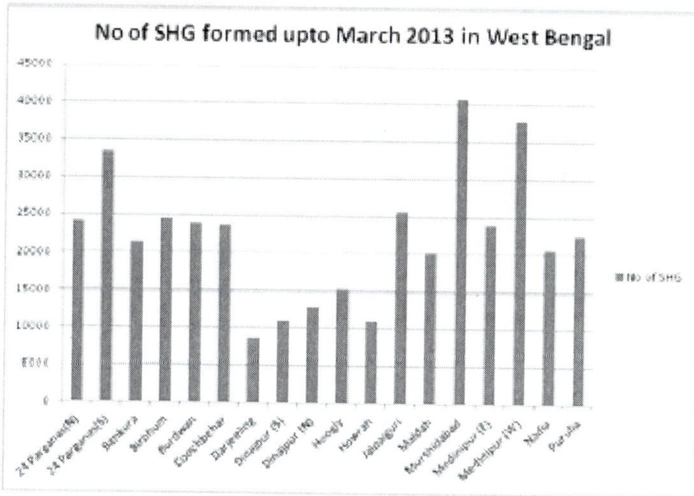

PHYSICAL PERFORMANCE OF THE RRBs IN MICROFINANCE

Now we open our analysis to our selected districts. Here we are able to collect the information up to March 2013. To judge the condition of physical achievements of the SHGs formed by RRBS in the two districts we have considered three parameters. They are total number of SHGs formed since inception, number of SHGs that have passed Grade I, number of SHGs that have passed Grade II. Tables 2 provide us the information according to our first parameter.

Table-2:Growth and Formation of SHGs by RRBs
(CoochBehar and Bankura)

Period (Since 1.4.99 to)	Group formed in CoochBehar		Group formed in Bankura	
	By RRB (UBK Gramin)	Growth of SHGs (compared to previous year)	By RRB (BGVB)	Growth of SHGs (compared to previous year)
Up to 2009	5126	------	6678	------
Up to 2010	6135	19.68	7565	13.28
Up to 2011	7002	14.13	8413	11.21
Up to 2012	8754	25.02	9175	9.06
Up to 2013	9176	4.82	10262	11.85

Source: Panchayat & Rural Development Department, WB

From the above table it is clear that UBK Gramin Bank of CoochBehar district shows better performance regarding the formation of SHGs compared to Bankura for the given years except the year 2013. We also calculate the rate of growth of the SHGs for the year 2013 considering 2009 as base year for the both the districts. The calculated value of the above mentioned growth rate stands at 79.00 percent and 53.67 percent for CoochBehar and Bankura respectively.

Fig.-2

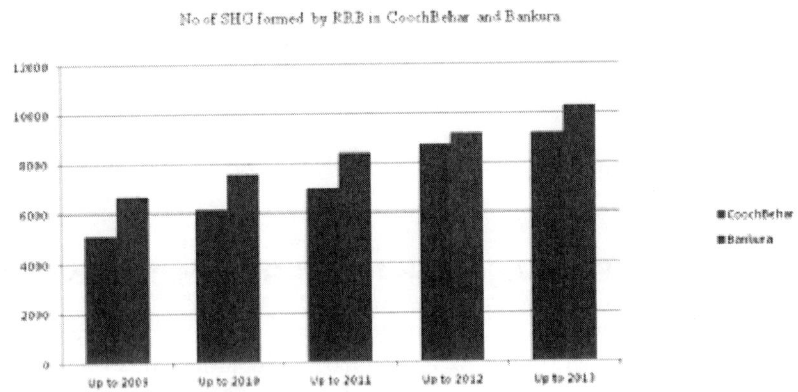

Again, Gradation is an important indicator to measure the performance of the groups already formed. For our selected districts the same performance of the SHGs is given in table 3 and 4 for Grade I and Grade II respectively. If we consider the percentage of groups that have passed Grade I and Grade II from Tables- 3 and 4, it is clear that the CoochBehar shows better performance for both I and II Gradation of the groups compared to Bankura. Not only that, we have also observed consistently higher percentage in CoochBehar compare to Bankura in case of both the number of SHG that have passed Grade I and Grade II.

Table-3: Number of SHGs that have passed Grade I
(CoochBehar and Bankura)

Period (Since 1.4.99 to)	CoochBehar			Bankura		
	Total no. of SHGs formed by UBK Gramin Bank	**No. of SHGs that have passed Grade I**	**In Percentage figure**	**Total no. of SHGs formed by BGVB**	**No. of SHGs that have passed Grade I**	**In Percentage figure**
Upto March 2009	5126	4058	79.17	6678	4176	62.53
Upto March 2010	6135	5302	86.42	7565	5778	76.38
Upto March 2011	7002	6595	94.19	8413	6459	76.77
Upto March 2012	8754	7929	90.58	9175	7414	80.81
Upto March 2013	9176	8236	89.76	10262	8465	82.49

Source: DRDC Cooch Behar & Bankura.

Fig.-3

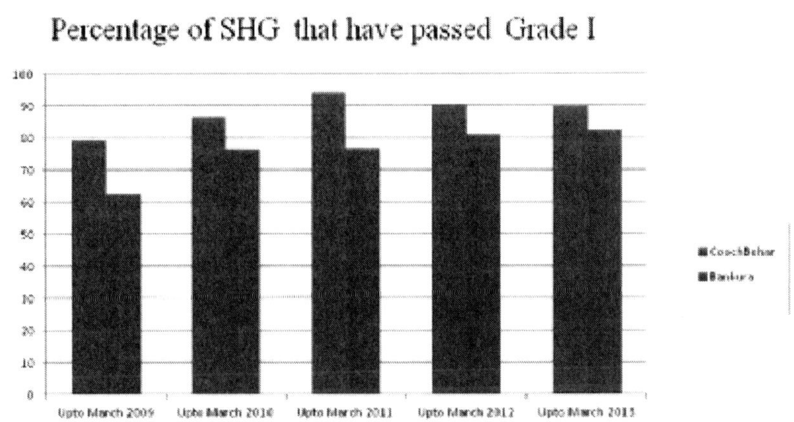

Table-4: Number of SHGs that have passed Grade II (CoochBehar and Bankura)

Period (Since 1.4.99 to)	CoochBehar			Bankura		
	Total no. of SHGs formed by UBK Gramin Bank	No. of SHGs that have passed Grade II	In Percentage figure	Total no. of SHGs formed by BGVB	No. of SHGs that have passed Grade II	In Percentage figure
Upto March 2009	5126	826	16.11	6678	624	9.34
Upto March 2010	6135	1504	24.52	7565	746	9.86
Upto March 2011	7002	1914	27.34	8413	1108	13.17
Upto March 2012	8754	2443	27.91	9175	1716	18.70
Upto March 2013	9176	2586	28.18	10262	2321	22.62

Source: DRDC Cooch Behar & Bankura.

Fig.-4

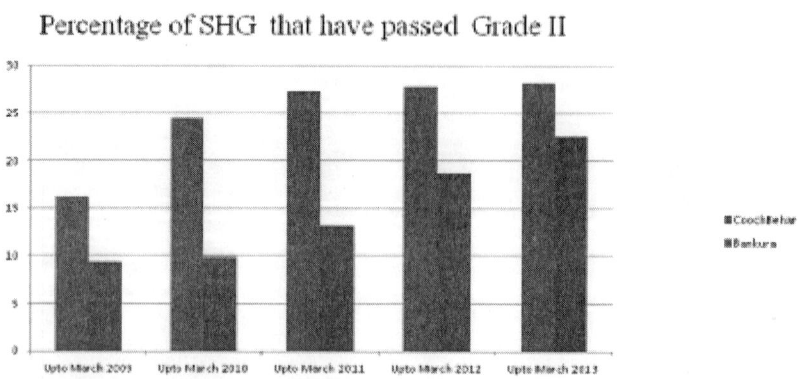

FINANCIAL PERFORMANCE OF THE RRBs IN MICROFINANCE

In this section we have tried to assess the overall financial performance of the SHGs of our Samples by the number of savings linked SHGs and by the number of credit link SHGs. In savings linked analysis importance has been given to per SHG savings and for credit link we have given importance to per SHG credit disbursement and per SHG member credit disbursement. All is given in tables 5 and 6 respectively. Again table 5 is being divided in 5A and 5B giving the information of saving link for CoochBehar and Bankura respectively. Similarly, table 6A and 6B provide us the credit link of the SHGs in our Sub-Samples.

If we consider the per SHG savings of our Sub-Samples considering the time frame up to March 2013 by RRBs, then we see that the SHGs of CoochBehar are succeeded to perform nearly five times more saving than the SHGs of Sub-Sample II. The other reference years also exhibits more or less the same kind of results. Again, if we have a look on disbursement of bank credit to SHGs by the regional rural banks (RRBs), then also we see that the SHGs of our first sample CoochBehar have succeeded to avail more amount of money as credit from the formal institutions compare to the SHGs of our second sample Bankura. On an average it figures to more than one and half times in our first sub-sample than our second sub-sample. Same is more or less true, as revealed from tables 6A and 6B, in case of credit disbursement to per SHG members also.

Table-5A: Saving A/C Linkage of SHGs
(CoochBehar)

Period (Since 1.4.99 to)	Savings Linked SHGs	Amount Saved (Rs. In Lakh)	Per SHG Saving(Rs.)
Upto March 2009	5126	413.49	8066.52
Upto March 2010	6135	1232.39	20087.85
Upto March 2011	7002	3872..42	55304.48
Upto March 2012	8754	3965.97	45304.67
Upto March 2013	9176	3987.07	43451.07

Source: DRDC Cooch Behar.

Table-5B: Saving A/C Linkage of SHGs
(Bankura)

Period (Since 1.4.99 to)	Savings Linked SHGs	Amount Saved (Rs. In Lakh)	Per SHG Saving (Rs)
Upto March 2009	6678	167.65	2510.48
Upto March 2010	7565	622.85	8233.31
Upto March 2011	8413	688.69	8186.02
Upto March 2012	9175	748.14	8154.11
Upto March 2013	10262	846.20	8245.95

Source: DRDC Bankura.

Fig.-5

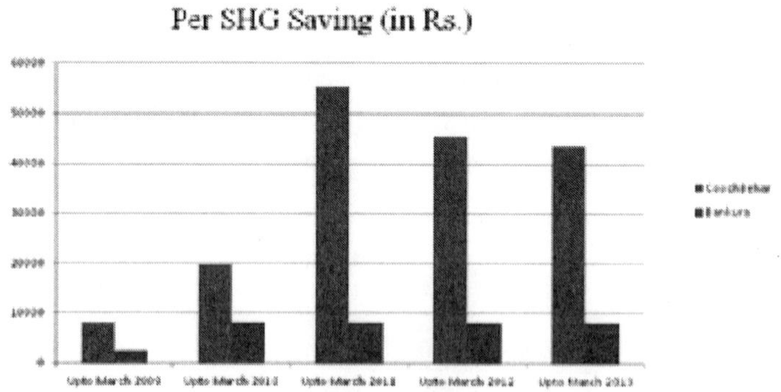

Table-6A: Cash Credit (C/C) Linkage of SHGs
(CoochBehar)

Period (Since 1.4.99 to)	Credit-Linked SHGs	No. of SHG members linked to credit	Amount Disbursed (Rs. In Lakh)	Per SHG disbursement (Rs.)	Per member disbursement (Rs.)
Upto March 2009	3002	29825	1036.40	34523.65	3474.94
Upto March 2010	3972	44655	1647.34	41473.82	3689.04
Upto March 2011	4988	53339	3537.17	70913.59	6631.49
Upto March 2012	5343	55368	3770.27	70564.66	6809.47
Upto March 2013	5655	59041	3998.03	70699.03	6771.62

Source: DRDC Cooch Behar.

Table-6B: Cash Credit (C/C) Linkage of SHGs
(Bankura)

Period (Since 1.4.99 to)	Credit-Linked SHGs	No. of SHG members linked to credit	Amount Disbursed (Rs. In Lakh)	Per SHG disbursement (Rs.)	Per member disbursement (Rs.)
Upto March 2009	3111	36726	435.63	14002.89	1186.16
Upto March 2010	5143	56539	2009.85	39079.33	3554.80
Upto March 2011	5777	62979	2280.47	39474.99	3621.00
Upto March 2012	6135	81762	2412.37	39321.43	2950.48
Upto March 2013	6665	92062	2620.65	39319.58	2846.61

Source: DRDC Bankura.

Fig.-6

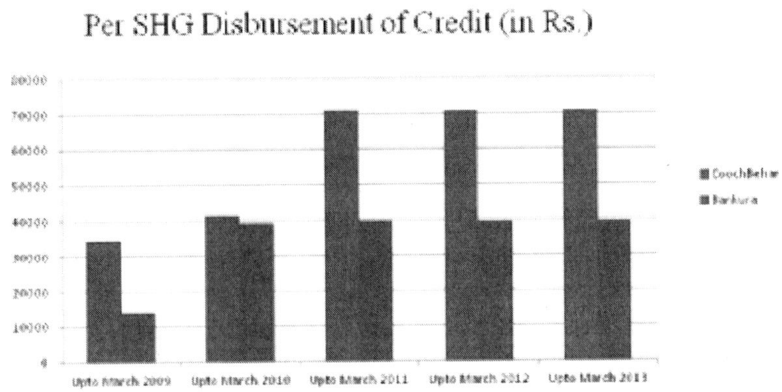

It is very clear from the preceding paragraphs that the in terms of facts and figures the working of the RRB in CoochBehar is quite good than the working of the RRB in Bankura.

SOME IMPORTANT FINDINGS AND CONCLUSION

From the above discussions we see that in terms of growth of SHGs our two Sub-Samples differ in a very high of level of percentage. If we make a comparison of growth of SHGs under SGSY by all the MFIs considering the time-frame 2009-2013 then we see that the two growth rates for CoochBehar and Bankura are 88.87 and 48.88 percent respectively. Same growth of SHGs by RRBs is 79.00 percent and 53.67 percent for CoochBehar and Bankura respectively. In both cases CoochBehar gains higher percentage. Again, the above facts permit us to conclude that the RRBs play an important role in rural microfinance under SGSY.

In case of the gradation of the SHGs formed by RRBs, we find higher percentage in case of our first Sub-Sample compared to our second Sub-Sample. The number of SHG that have passed Grade-I in CoochBehar up to March 2009 is 79.17 percent. The same for Bankura in same reference period stands at 62.53 percent. Again, if we consider the time frame up to March 2013 then the two percentage figure becomes 89.76 and 82.49 respectively for CoochBehar and Bankura. We also observed consistently higher percentage in CoochBehar compare to Bankura in case of number of SHG that have passed Grade II. Finally, per SHG saving, per SHG loan disbursement and per SHG member loan disbursement all are again consistently very high in CoochBehar in comparison to Bankura.

Thus we can say, on the basis of above inferences that although RRBs play vital role in rural microfinance but the SHG movement by RRB is not uniform across the districts of West Bengal. This is true for our Sub-Samples also. Bankura is lagging behind of CoochBehar in all respects of our chosen indicators. But what remains to say here is that in spite of higher SHG saving in CoochBehar the per SHG credit disbursement is not so high in CoochBehar.

REFERENCES

Amin, S. and Pebley, A. R. (1994), "Gender Inequality within Households: The impact of a women's development programme in thirty six Bangladeshi villages", The Bangladesh Development Studies, xxii (2&3), pp. 121-154.

Bagchi, K. K. and Sarkar, S. (2003), "Development of Social Sector in West Bengal: A Study in Inter District Disparity", Indian Journal of Regional Science, Vol. 35, No.2, pp.115-130.

Dasgupta, R. (2006), "An Architectural Plan for a Micro Finance Institutional Net Work", EPW, Vol. 41, March 18.

Harper, M. (1998), Profit for Poor, Oxford University Press.

Jayaraman, R. (2002), "Role of Self Help Groups in Fisherwomen Development in India", paper presented at the Coastal Zone Asia Pacific Conference, 12-16, May, 2002, Bangkok, Thailand.

Kabeer, N. (2005), "Is Micro Finance is a Magic Bullet for Women Empowerment? Analysis from Findings from South Asia", Economic and Political Weekly, Vol. XL, No 44-45.

Kumaran, K. P. (1997), Self Help Groups – alternative of Institutional credit for the poor: A case study in Andhra Pradesh, Journal of Rural Development, Vol.16, No.3, PP. 515-530.

Kurukshetra, Vol.54, No. 11, PP 14-16.

Loganathan and Asokan (2006), "Inter Regional Development of Self Help Groups in India" Kurukshetra, Vol.54, No. 11, PP 9-12.

Mayoux, L. (1997), "The Magic Ingredient? "Microfinance and Women's Empowerment", A briefing paper prepared for Micro Credit Summit, Washington.

MYRADA (2002), Impact of Self-help Groups on the social/empowerment status of women members in Southern India, NABARD, Mumbai.

NABARD (2003-2006), "Progress of SHG-Bank Linkage in India2 2002-03", Mumbai

Satish, P. (2001), Some Issues in the formation of Self Help Groups, Indian Journal of Agricultural Economics, Vol.56, No.3

Sen, M. (2005), Study of Self Help Group and Micro Finance in West Bengal, SIPRD, Kalyani.

Sharma, A. (2000), "Developing Sustainable Micro-credit System", Asian Development Bank Report, 1998 to 2000.

Soundarapandian (2006), "Micro Finance for Rural Entrepreneurs-Issues and Strategies".

Sundar and Asokan (2004), "Regional Variation in Performance of Self Help Groups" Social Welfare, January 2004.

Swope, T. (2005), "Microfinance and poverty alleviation", http://www.creativecommons.org./ licenses/by-ne-sa/3.

World Bank (2003), Microfinance in India: Issues, Challenges and Policy Options, Washington DC, World Bank.

Zaman, H. (2001), "Assessing the poverty and vulnerability impact of microcredit in Bangladesh: A case study of BRAC", unpublished background paper for World Bank, World Development Report 2000/2001, Washington.

15

Regional Rural Banks in India: Problems and Current Scenario

Subrata Jana
Sukhen Kali
Rabindranath De Dalal

INTRODUCTION

After nationalization of commercial banks (1969) and establishment of Regional Rural Banks in 1975 both the categories of banks are extending credit facilities for agricultural purpose. As agriculture sector contributes about 40% of worldwide employment and a 100% food production increase will be required in developing countries to feed the 2050 population. Technology playing an important role in the management of high yielding variety seeds has increased productivity of crops considerably.

The need in agriculture now is a new mission mode akin to what was done in the 1970s with the Green Revolution. The difference now is that initiatives are needed in a disaggregated manner in many different segments of agriculture and agro-industry: horticulture, aquaculture, pisciculture, dairying, sericulture, poultry, vegetables, meat and food processing, other agro-processing. In order to reach the poorest in rural India it ensures credit and financial services for small and marginal farmers.

The rural credit market consists of both formal and informal financial institutions and agencies that meet the credit needs of the cultivators in India. The informal sector advances loans at very high rate of interest; the terms and conditions attached to such loans have given rise to an elaborate structure of intimidation of economic and non-economic conditions in the rural population of India.

STRUCTURE OF RRBs

Regional Rural Banks in India date back to the years 1975. It's the Narasimham Committee that conceptualized the foundation of Regional Rural Banks in India. The committee felt the need of regionally oriented rural banks that would address the problems and requirements of the rural people in India. Regional Rural Banks were established under the provisions of an ordinance promulgated on the 26th September 1975 and the RRB Act, 1975 with an objective to ensure sufficient institutional credit for agriculture and other rural sectors. The RRBs mobilize financial resources from rural/ semi urban areas and grant loans and advances mostly to small and marginal farmers, agricultural laborers and rural artisans. The objectives of RRB are summarized as to provide cheap and liberal credit facilities to small and marginal farmers, agriculture, to save the rural poor from the money lenders, to act as a catalyst element and thereby accelerate the economic growth in the particular region.

STRUCTURE OF AGRICULTURAL CREDIT SYSTEM IN INDIA

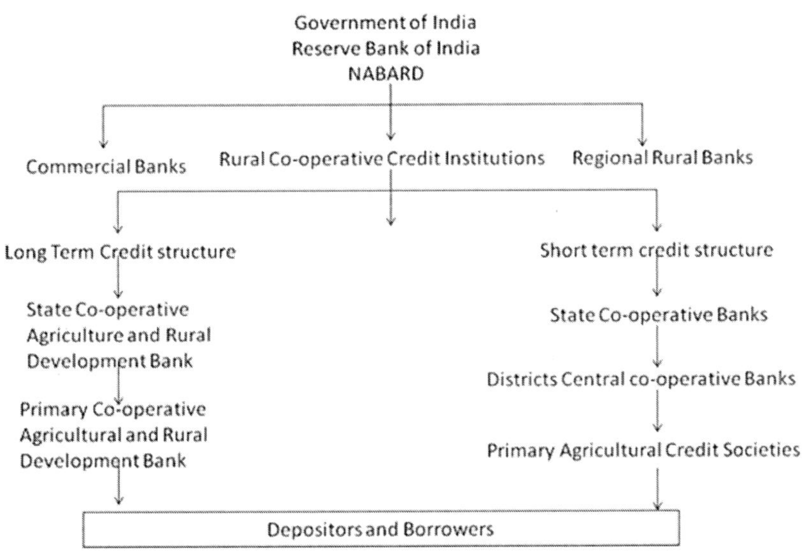

Source: RBI

Problems:

Major problems faced by regional rural banks are as follows:

Rigidities:

The RRBs follow the procedures of the scheduled commercial banks in the matter of deposits and advancing loans which are highly complicated and time-consuming from the villagers' point of view. The rural borrowers always appreciate informal ways and simple procedures as have been followed by the money-lenders and the indigenous bankers.

Deposit Mobilisation:

The RRBs exclude the richer sections of the village society in providing direct financial assistance. These sections have potential savings to deposit. But, they are least interested in depositing them with the RRBs in view of the restrictive credit policy of these banks. Further, state and local governments and their agencies also have not co-operated much by maintaining their deposit accounts with the RRBs.

Limited scope of investment:

The basic objective of RRBs was to provide credit facilities to poor and weaker sections of society, i.e., to small and marginal farmers and other weaker sections. They were originally having limited scope to invest their surplus funds freely.

Slow progress:

The progress of RRBs is not up to the expectation and is slow when comparing with other types of banks because of many restrictions on their operations. For example till 1996, RRBS were permitted to lend only under priority sector schemes.

Decision making:

The RRBs are controlled directly and indirectly by various agencies, i.e., the sponsoring bank, NABARD, RBI, besides Central Government. Thus, it takes long time to take decisions on some important issues. This, in turn affects the progress of RRBs. However, since end 1997, the operational responsibility of RRBs has been passed on to sponsor bank.

Some performance indicator of RRBs

	As on 31.03.2013	As on 31.03.2014
No. of RRBs	64	57
Share Capital (in Rs. Crore)	197	197
Share Capital Deposit (in Rs. Crore)	6001	6170
Reserves (in Rs. Crore)	13247	15262
Profit Earning RRBs	64	57
Net Profit of of RRBs (in Rs. Crore)	2273	2744
Accumulated Losses (in Rs. Crore)	1091	949
Deposits (in Rs. Crore)	211488	239511
Loan and Advances (in Rs. Crore)	137078	218110
Non Performing Loans	6.08	4.35

PRESENT SCENARIO

There are 8 RRBs whose accumulated losses had increased by 17% as on 31st March 2014 over the previous year. The aggregate reserves of RRBs increased to Rs.15736 crore and net worth increased to Rs.21199 crore in 2013-14. The provisional financial results of RRBs for the financial year 2013-14 indicates that all 57 RRBs have earned profits aggregating Rs.2833 crore. The aggregate deposits of RRBs registered a growth of 13 percent, borrowings 34 percent, investment 2 percent in the financial year 2013-14 over the previous year.

CONCLUSION

India is primary agricultural and densely populated rural country compared with urban areas, which needs the financial assistance as well as rural friendly, policies to develop rural areas. The RRBs are playing a vital role in the development of rural and needy agriculture poor people in all spheres. The Bangiya Gramin Bank is one of the growing banks in West Bengal to serve the poor agricultural farmers. The Bank will expand its branches all over the rural areas in West Bengal to assists the farmer's financial plight. There is a consistent improvement in all the thrust areas of the bank.

SUGGESTIONS

RRBs need ATMs in the rural areas as well as urban areas to enhance their Services. RRBs can expand its services through post offices for financial transactions in the rural areas. In view of food security bill there is a need to increase the production of pulses and cereals under circumstances. The RRBs should come to the support of small and medium farmers who are the back bone of Indian agriculture and national economy.

REFERENCES

1. Annual Report RRB 2012-13, 2013-14
2. Regional rural banks-problems and prospects A case study". Financing agriculture, 14(2), April-June, 1984, New Delhi, pp54-56.
3. www.nabard.org
4. Murthy, N.P.S.V.N., Devi, Dr. M.Sarada, Performance of Regional Rural Banks in India during post merger period, International Journal of Cademic Research, July-sept. 2014.
5. Rao, B. Venkata, Rao, Dr. G. Sudarasana, Performance of Regional Rural Banks inIndia A Study on Andhra Pradesh Gramin Vikash Bank in Andhra Pradesh, International Journal of Advance Research in Computer science and Management Studies, April 2014.

16

Financial Viability and Potentiality of Regional Rural Banks in India

Probhat Kumar Pal

INTRODUCTION

Bank plays an important role in generation and allocation of resources in any country. Rural people are facing problems in the inadequate supply of institutional credit facilities. They are compelled to take credit from informal sources with high rate of interest. They are exploited by the Mahajans or money lenders. RRBs were established to mitigate the sufferings of the rural people by extending credit facilities with minimum rate of interest. The objectives were to develop the rural economy through extending credit facilities in the field of agriculture, trade commerce, industry, other productive activities, credit and other facilities to the small and marginal farmers, agricultural labourers, artisans and small entrepreneurs. The objectives of this study are to analyse the financial viability and potentiality of the RRBs in respect of capital structure and profitability.

AN OVERVIEW OF INDIAN REGIONAL RURAL BANKS

Regional Rural Banks were established under the provisions of an Ordinance promulgated on the 26th September 1975 and the RRB Act, 1975 with an objective to ensure sufficient institutional credit for agriculture and other rural sectors. The RRBs generate financial resources grant loans and advances mostly to small and marginal farmers, agricultural laborers and rural artisans. The Narasimham committee conceptualized the foundation of Regional Rural Bank in India. The committee recommended the formation of regionally oriented rural bank to address the sufferings of the rural people.

In 1991-92, during financial sector reforms to strengthen RRBs and improve their performance many initiatives have been taken by the Government of India and the Reserve Bank of India (RBI) and comprehensive restructuring programme, recapitalization of RRBs were initiated in the year 1994-95. Aggregate financial support of Rs.2188.44 crore from the shareholders, viz., Government of India, State Governments and sponsor Banks in the ratio of 50:15:35 was extended. The branches of RRBs may conduct foreign exchange business with the prior approval of the concerned Government authority and RBI. These banks have also been allowed to open extension counters at the premises of the institutions of which they are principal bankers after obtaining license from the concerned regional office of the RBI.

METHODOLOGY OF THE STUDY

The present study is based on secondary data available from different sources. The relevant secondary data have been collected mainly from the data bases of Reserve Bank of India (RBI), National Bank for Agricultural and Rural Development (NABARD). The study is confined only to the specific areas like number of branches, district coverage, owned capital, debt capital, profit, outstanding loan and non-performing assets etc. In order to analyze the data and draw conclusions in this study, various statistical tools like compound rate of growth, correlation between the two variables and regression equations have been applied.

Table-1: Number of Regional Rural Banks

Year	No of RRBs	No of Branches	District Covered	Staff Involved
2011-12	82	16909	638	74291
2012-13	84	17861	635	76246
2013-14	57	19082	642	80075

Source: Central Statiscal Information Department (NABARD)

The number of RRBs has decreased because of amalgamation process initiated by the Govt. of India for recapitalization and to give operational freedom to the RRBs. The compound rate of growth of branches is 0 .06 which indicates that no of branches increased by 6% over the years under consideration. No of staff increased by 3% over the years (compound rate of growth is 0.03).

CAPITAL STRUCTURE

Capital structure indicates composition of capital consisting of owned capital and debt capital. Owned capital comprises of share capital, share capital deposits and reserves and surpluses and debt capital comprises of borrowings from NABARD, Sponsor banks and others.

Table-2: Capital Structure (Rs. in Crore)

Year	Owned Capital (Rs.)	Debt Capital (Rs.)	Total Capital (Rs.)	Net Profit (Rs.)
2011-12	16462	30289	46751	1857
2012-13	19445	38073	57518	2273
2013-14	22103	51208	73311	2694

Source: Central Statiscal Information Department (NABARD)

From Table 2, it is found that compound rate of growth of equity capital and debt capital are 0.16(16%), and 0.30(30%) respectively. Compound rate of return on equity capital, debt capital express that equity capital increase by 16% and 30% respectively over the years. The total amount of net profit is very worse. Compound rate of growth of net profit is 0 .20(20%) over the years. Compound rate of growth of total capital indicates that capital increases 25% over the years, which is very significant. Rate of growth of debt capital is more than that of equity capital that will be better if there is trading on equity regarding utilization of debt capital; otherwise there will be negative impact on the rate of return to the equity holders.

The correlation coefficient (r) between equity capital and net profit is found to be 0.99 and =0.99 which implies that in 99% cases when equity capital changes net profit also changes. As there is relevant relationship and no trend factor, the correlation is not spurious. There is positive correlation between the two variables. The correlation coefficient (r) between debt capital and net profit is 0.98 and =0.97, which indicates that in 97% cases net profit increases due to increase in debt capital, they are positively correlated. The correlation between total capital and net profit is 0.99 and =0.98. It implies that in 98% cases net profit increases due to increase in total capital.

Through regression analysis we can estimate the value of one variable when the value of other variable is given. The regression equation of net profit (y i.e. dependent variable) on equity capital (x i.e. independent variable) is y-= (x- where is mean value of y values and is mean value of x values i.e. equity capital and is the slope or regression coefficient of y on x. The slope of the equation is positive (0.148), which means that if equity increases by one unit (Rs. 1 lakh) net profit also increases by Rs. 14800. =0.99 indicates that in 99% cases one variable increases as the other variable increases. Positive relation between equity capital and net profit indicates that capital is utilized to earn profit but the volume of profit is not satisfactory.

The slope of the regression equation of net profit on debt capital is 0.039 which indicates that if debt capital increases by one lakh profit will increase by Rs.3900. Profit increases due to positive regression slope. =0.97 indicates that in 97% cases net profit increases when debt capital increases. The positive regression slope is found in case of regression equation of net profit on total capital. The regression slope 0.031 indicates that if total capital increases by one lakh net profit increases by Rs. 3100 and =0.98 indicates that in 98% cases net profit increases as total capital increases. In every cases profit increases but the magnitude of increase is not up to the satisfaction. It is observed that major portion of profit is required to meet the fixed obligation.

SHORT-TERM LIQUIDITY

Liquidity refers to the debt paying ability of a society. Short-term liquidity of the bank means the capability of the bank to meet the short term obligation. There should be sufficient current assets to pay the current liabilities. If current assets is excessive than its requirements it will lead to idle capacity of current assets. So current assets should be appropriate to handle the current liabilities. Cash and bank balance is more liquid than other components of current assets. Absence of liquidity leads to financial insecurity in the market. Even a high degree of liquidity is not good because such a situation represents unnecessarily excessive funds being tied up in the form of current assets.

Table-3: Current assets and current liabilities (Rs. In Crore)

Year	Current Assets	Current Liability	Working Capital	Net Profit
2011-12	58943	195783	136840	1857
2012-13	73560	221975	148415	2273
2013-14	86361	249266	162905	2694

Source: Central Statistical Information Department (NABARD)

Compound rate of growth of current assets is 0.21(21%), compound rate of growth of current liabilities is 0.12(12%) and compound rate of growth of working capital is 0.09(9%). It indicates that current assets, current liabilities and working capital increase 21%, 12% and 9% over the years. The rate of increase of working capital is slow comparing the need of the demand.

The degree of association between working capital and net profit is 0.99 and =0.99 which indicates that in 99% cases net profit increases when working capital increases and the vice-versa.

The positive regression slope is found in case of regression equation of net profit on working capital. The regression slope 0.031 indicates that if working capital increases by one lakh net profit increases by Rs. 3100 and = 0.99 indicates that in 99% cases net profit increases as working capital increases but the degree of increase is not significant. It means that either working capital is insufficient or it is not properly utilized.

PROFITABILITY

The primary objective of a RRB is to earn profits. Earning capacity means the profit earning capability of a bank. Bank having earning more profit will sustain longer keeping secured its capital. Profit is essential for survival and growth of a bank. An investor wants an adequate return on his investments. A RRB can discharge its obligations to the various interested groups of the society through its earnings. Thus, profit is a useful measure of overall efficiency of a bank.

Table-4: Profitability (Rs. in Crore)

Year	Total No of RRBs	RRBs in Profit	RRBs in Loss	Net Profit
2009-10	82	79	3	1884
2010-11	82	75	7	1715
2011-12	82	79	3	1857
2012-13	64	63	1	2273
2013-14	57	57	0	2694

Source: Central Statistical Information Department (NABARD)

Compound rate of growth of net profit is 0.10 (10%) which implies that net profit increases 10% over the years. Though most of the RRBs are under in profitability yet the volume of profit and its growth is not satisfactory.

CREDIT FLOW TO AGRICULTURE

Amount of loan extended to the small and marginal farmers for rural agricultural development.

Table-5: Credit Flow to Agriculture (Rs. In Crore)

Year	RRBs	% Share to Total	Other Banks	% Share to Total	Total Loan
2009-10	35218	9.16	349297	90.84	384515
2010-11	44293	9.46	423998	90.54	468291
2011-12	54450	10.65	456579	89.35	511029
2012-13	63681	10.48	543695	89.52	607376
2013-14	82653	11.61	628969	88.39	711622

Source: Central Statistical Information Department (NABARD)

Compound rate of growth loan extended by the RRBs is .23(23%) i.e. amount of loan increases by 23% over the years and it is 16% in case of total amount of loan extended by the banks to the rural sector. Regarding percentage of loan extension it is 10% on an average in comparison to other banks.

CONCLUSION

Regional Rural Banks were established by the Government of India to emancipate the rural people from the clutches of informal money lenders by developing and revitalizing the village economy. It helps to reduce the regional disparities in respect of banking facilities in India. With the passage of time the role of RRBs in mobilizing deposits, rural development, branch expansions, and credit deployment to the agriculture sector and the weaker section of rural areas are on the growing stage. The rate of growth of number of people involved in the RRBs, owned Capital, debt capital, net profit, amount of loan extended to the poor people are satisfactory. The role of RRBs regarding loan disbursement in comparison to other banks is increasing gradually. Although the agricultural flow is good but the small and marginal farmers are unable to avail credit easily. RRBs should properly utilize the capital and deposit mobilized for the betterment of the rural people and the Govt. should extend enough freedom within the ambit of its financial control to regulate RRBs to mitigate the sufferings of the rural people.

REFERENCES

1. Government of India Report of the Committee on Rural Banks, (Chairman-M, Narasimhan), New Delhi, 1975.
2. NABARD (2013), Annual Report 201-12, 2012-13, National Bank for Agriculture and Rural Development, Head Office, Mumbai.
3. Narasimhan Committee, 1991. Report of the Committee on the Financial System, Government of India.
4. RBI (2004):„Report of the Advisory Committee on Flow of Credit to Agriculture and Related Activities from the Banking System (Chairman: V S Vyas) Reserve Bank of India, Mumbai.
5. NABARD, Consolidated Review of Performance of Regional Rural Banks.

17

Regional Rural Banks in India: Challenges and Prospects

Mantu Kumar Das

INTRODUCTION

Rural people in India such as small and marginal farmers, landless agricultural labourers have been exploited in the name of credit facility by informal sectors. The rural credit market consists of both formal and informal financial institutions and agencies that meet the credit needs of the cultivators in India. The informal sector advances loans at very high rate of interest; the terms and conditions attached to such loans have given rise to an elaborate structure of intimidation of economic and non-economic conditions in the rural population of India. The supply of total formal credit is inadequate and rural credit is inadequate. Rural credit markets are imperfect and fragmented. Regional Rural Banks in India date back to the year 1975. It's the Narasimham Committee that conceptualized the foundation of Regional Rural Banks in India. The committee felt the need of regionally oriented rural banks that would address the problems and requirements of the rural people in India. Regional Rural Banks were established under the provisions of an ordinance promulgated on 26th September 1975 and the RRB Act, 1975 with an objective to ensure sufficient institutional credit for agriculture and other rural sectors. The RRBs mobilize financial resources from rural/ semi urban areas and grant loans and advances mostly to small and marginal farmers, agricultural labourers and rural artisans. The objectives of RRB are summarized as to provide cheap and liberal credit facilities to small and marginal farmers, agriculture, to save the rural poor from the money lenders, to act as a catalyst element and there by accelerate the economic growth in the particular region. Regional rural Banks play a vital role in the agriculture and rural development of India. The RRBS have more reached to the rural area of India, through their huge network. The success of rural credit in India is largely depends on their financial strength. RRBs are key financing institution at the rural level which shoulders responsibility of meeting credit needs of different types of agriculture credit in rural areas. At present, most of the regional rural banks are facing the problems of overdue, recovery, nonperforming assets and other problems.

REGIONAL RURAL BANKS: CHALLENGES AND PROSPECTS

Regional Rural Banks have been in existence for around three decades in the Indian financial scenario. Inception of regional rural banks (RRBs) can be seen as a unique experiment as well as experience in improving the rural credit delivery mechanism in India. With joint share holding by Central Government, the concerned State Government and the sponsoring bank an effort was made to integrate commercial banking within the broad policy thrust towards social banking keeping in view the local demand. The genesis of the Regional Rural Banks can be traced to the need for a stronger institutional arrangement for providing rural credit. The Narasimham committee conceptualised the creation of RRBs in 1975 as a new set of regionally oriented rural banks. Subsequently, the RRBs were set up through the promulgation of RRB Act of 1976. Their equity is held by the Central Government, concerned State Government and the Sponsor Bank in the proportion of 50:15:35. RRBs were supposed to evolve as specialised rural financial institutions for developing the rural economy by providing credit to small and marginal farmers, agricultural labourers and small entrepreneurs. Over the years, the RRBs have taken deep roots and have become a sort of inseparable part of the rural credit structure. They have played a key role in rural institutional financing in terms of geographical coverage and business volume as also contribution to the development of the rural economy. A remarkable feature of their performance over the past three decades has been the massive expansion of their retail network in rural areas. From a modest beginning of 6 RRBs with 17 branches covering 12 districts in December 1975, the numbers have grown into 196 RRBs with 14,446 branches working in 518 districts across the country in March 2004. RRBs have a large branch network in the rural area forming around 43 per cent of the total rural branches of commercial banks.

PROBLEMS FACED BY REGIONAL RURAL BANKS IN INDIA

Banks have higher non-performing loans in rural areas because of irregular income and expenditure patterns. The issue is compounded by the dependence of the rural economy on monsoons, and loan waivers driven by Governments. NPLs from the agriculture sector are 7.7%, compared to 3.5% across non-agriculture sectors. In order for banks to view rural India as a growth opportunity, rather than a regulatory requirement, a combination of these issues must be addressed. Increasing financial access to rural areas is contingent upon basic conditions such as proper infrastructure and an enabling regulatory framework, as well as innovative thinking on the part of commercial banks. The average ticket size of both a deposit transaction and a credit transaction in rural areas is small. Considering the small catchments area of a branch in rural areas, generating a customer base with critical mass is challenging. Branches are the only used channel in rural areas. This is because many rural people are not literate and are not comfortable using technology-driven channels such as ATMs, mobile banking or internet banking. At present, most of the regional rural banks are facing the problems of overdue, recovery, nonperforming assets and other problems.

CONCLUSIONS

The rapid expansion of RRB has helped in reducing the regional disparities in respect of banking facilities in India. The efforts made by RRB in branch expansion, deposit mobilization, rural development and credit deployment in weaker section of rural areas are appreciable. RRB successfully achieve its objectives like to take banking to door steps of rural households particularly in banking deprived rural area, to avail easy and cheaper credit to weaker rural section who are dependent on private lenders, to encourage rural savings for productive activities, to generate employment in rural areas and to bring down the cost of purveying credit in rural areas. Thus RRB is providing the strongest banking network. of loan & high risk in loan & advances. Rural banks need to remove lack of transparency in their operation which leads to unequal relationship between banker and customer. Banking staff should interact more with their customers to overcome this problem. Banks should open their branches in areas where customers are not able to avail banking facilities. Presently most of the regional rural banks are facing the problems of overdue, recovery, nonperforming assets and other problems.

REFERENCES

1. Bagachi, K. K. and A. Hadi (2006), Performance of Regional Rural Banks in West Bengal: an evaluation, Serials Publications: New Delhi.
2. Bose, S. (2005) Regional Rural Banks: The Past and the Present Debate
3. Gupta, S.K (1996) "Profitability and Regional Rural Banks", Kurukshetra, July.
4. Horseman, S.B (2002), Performance of Regional Rural Banks, New Delhi,
5. Khankhoje, D. and Sathye, M. (2008) "Efficiency of Rural Banks: The Case of India", International Business Research, Vol. 1. No.2, pp. 140-149. 10. Kannan, R. (2004), Regional Rural Banks.

Contributors

ARUN KUMAR ROY, Principal, Barjora College, Barjora, Bankura, West Bengal, India

BHAJAN CHANDRA BARMAN, Assistant Professor, Department of Economics, Netaji Nagar College, Kolkata, West Bengal, India

CHITTARANJAN SARKAR, Former Professor, Department of Commerce, The University of Burdwan, Golapbag, Burdwan, West Bengal, India

DEBASISH BISWAS, Assistant Professor, Department of Business Administration, Vidyasagar University, West Bengal, India

DEBASISH SUR, Professor, Department of Commerce, The University of Burdwan, Golapbag, Burdwan, West Bengal, India

DHANONJOY KUMAR, Associate Professor, Department of Management, Islamic University, Kushtia, Bangladesh

DHIREN PAL, Former Associate Professor, Department of Economics, Dr. Gour Mohan Roy College, Monteswar, Burdwan, West Bengal, India

GOUTAM CHATTERJEE, Principal, Hetampur K.C. College, Hetampur, Birbhum, West Bengal, India

GOUTAM SINHA, Assistant Professor, Department of Humanities, Bankura Unnayani Institute of Engineering, Subhankar Nagar, Puabagan, Bankura, West Bengal, India

JAYDEB SARKHEL, Former Professor, Department of Commerce, University of Burdwan, Golapbag, Burdwan, West Bengal, India.

KRISHNA SINGH, Assistant Professor, Department of Economics, University of Gour Banga, Malda, West Bengal, India

MANTU KUMAR DAS, Associate Professor, Department of Physics, Garhbeta College, Paschim Medinipur, West Bengal, India

PANKAJ KUMAR PAUL, Assistant Professor, Department of Education, Gourav Guin Memorial College, Paschim Medinipur, West Bengal, India

PARTHA PRATIM ROY, Assistant Professor, Department of Commerce, Mahatma Gandhi College, Lalpur, Purulia, West Bengal, India

PINTU PRASAD JAISWAL, Assistant Professor, Department of Commerce, KGTM College, Bagdogra, West Bengal, India

PROBHAT KUMAR PAL, Assistant Professor, Department of Commerce, Rishi Bankim Chandra College, Naihati, West Bengal, India

RABINDRANATH DE DALAL, Assistant Professor, Department of Commerce, Bankura Sammilani College, Bankura, West Bengal, India

RATUL SAHA, Assistant Professor, Department of Economics, Sonamukhi College, Bankura, West Bengal, India

SAMIRENDRA NATH DHAR, Professor, Department of Commerce, University of North Bengal, Darjeeling, West Bengal, India

SANTOSH KONER, Associate Professor, Department of Commerce, Chatra Ramai Pandit Mahavidyalaya, Bankura, West Bengal, India

SIDDHARTHA BHADRA, Assistant Professor, Department of Economics, M.U.C. Women's College, Burdwan, West Bengal, India

SK. ATAUR RAHAMAN, Assistant Professor, Department of Commerce, Chandidas Mahvidyalaya, Khujutipara, Birbhum, West Bengal, India

SUBRATA JANA, Assistant Professor, Department of Commerce, Bankura Sammilani College, Bankura, West Bengal, India

SUKHEN KALI, Assistant Professor, Department of Commerce, Bankura Sammilani College, Bankura, West Bengal, India

SWAPAN KUMAR BISWAS, Former Associate Professor, Department of Commerce, Khatra Adibasi Mahavidyalaya, Khatra, Bankura, West Bengal, India

TANAY KUMAR PAL, Associate Professor, Department of Commerce, Dr. Gour Mohan Roy College, Monteswar, Burdwan, West Bengal, India

UDAY CHAND DAS, Associate Professor, Department of Commerce, Ramananda College, Bishnupur, Bankura, West Bengal, India

UTTAM KUMAR DUTTA, Professor, Department of Commerce, West Bengal State University, Barasat, Kolkata, West Bengal, India